11/09 Natalie W Turner

MW00966323

The Christian's Children's SONGBOOK

ISBN 978-1-4234-3507-5

HAL•LEONARD®
CORPORATION
7777 W. BLUEMOUND RD. P.O. BOX 13819 MILWAUKEE, WI 53213

Visit Hal Leonard Online at
www.halleonard.com

Contents

ALL NIGHT, ALL DAY

Spiritual

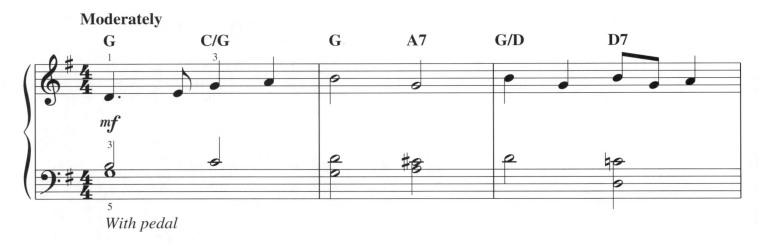

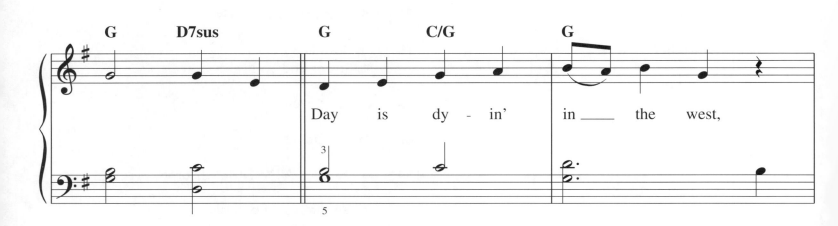

Day is dy - in' in ____ the west,

An - gels watch-in' o - ver me, my Lord; _ Sleep, my child, and

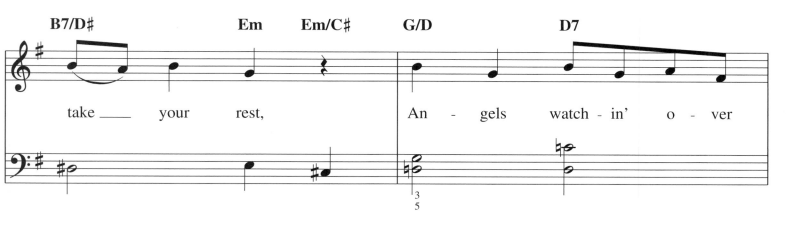

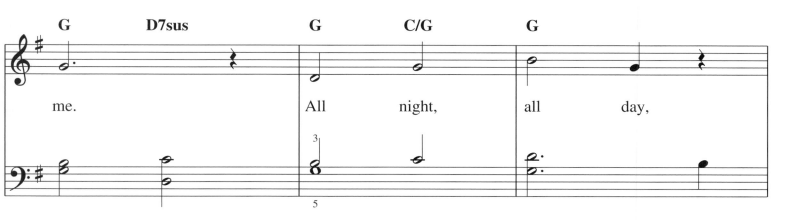

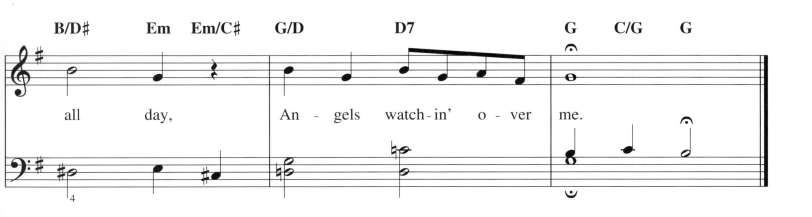

ALL THINGS BRIGHT AND BEAUTIFUL

Words by CECIL FRANCES ALEXANDER
17th Century English Melody

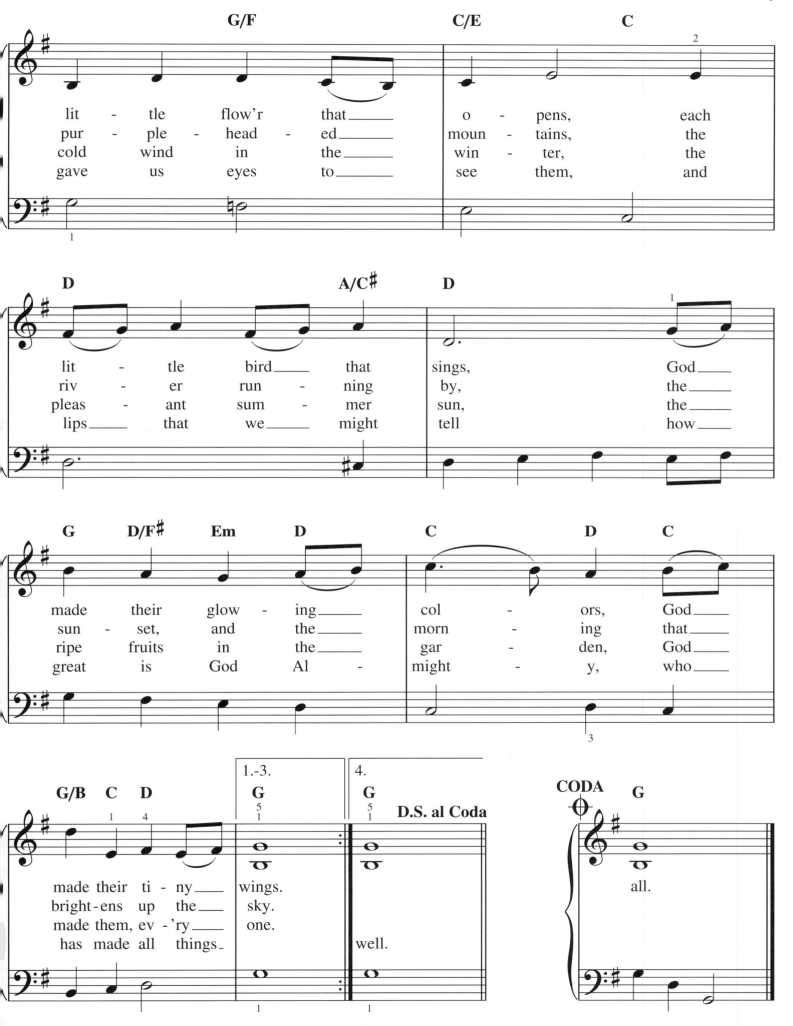

AWESOME GOD

Words and Music by
RICH MULLINS

CELEBRATE JESUS

Words and Music by
GARY OLIVER

12

THE BIBLE TELLS ME SO

Words and Music by
DALE EVANS

14

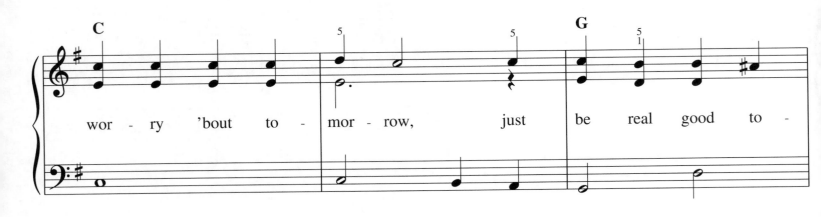

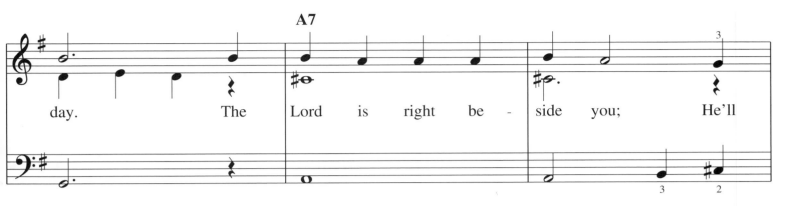

day. The Lord is right be - side you; He'll

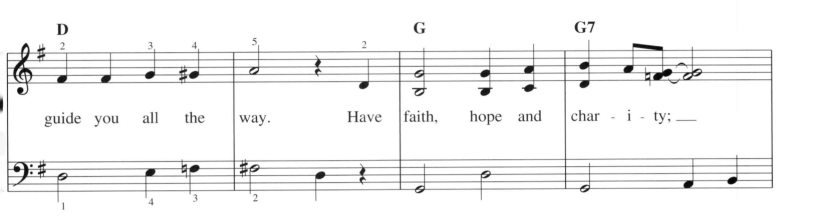

guide you all the way. Have faith, hope and char - i - ty; ___

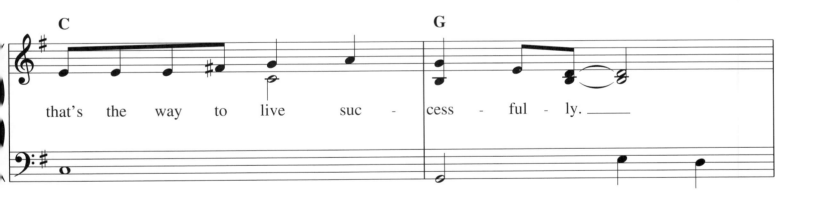

that's the way to live suc - cess - ful - ly. ___

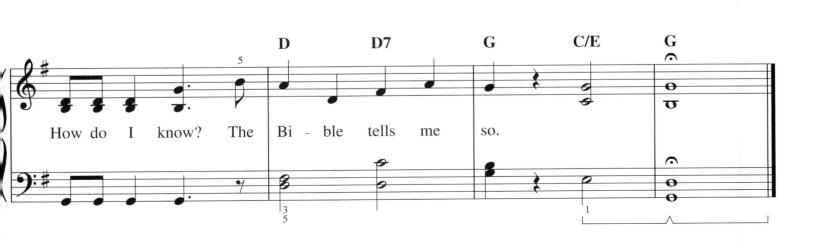

How do I know? The Bi - ble tells me so.

CLAP YOUR HANDS

Words and Music by JIMMY OWENS
Text Based on Psalm 47:1

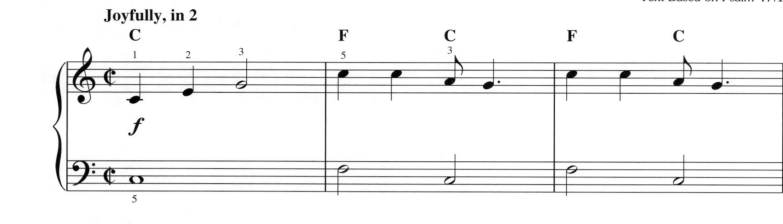

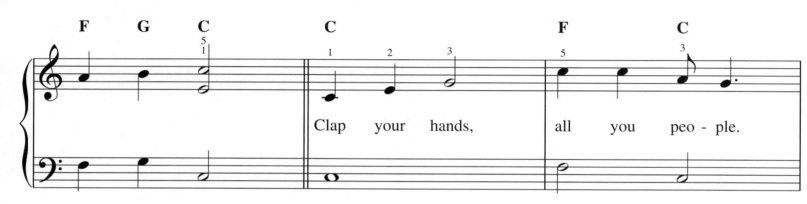

Clap your hands, all you peo - ple.

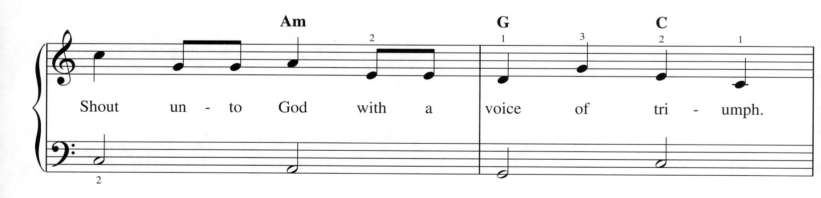

Shout un - to God with a voice of tri - umph.

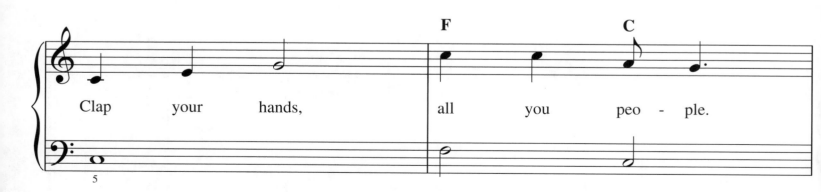

Clap your hands, all you peo - ple.

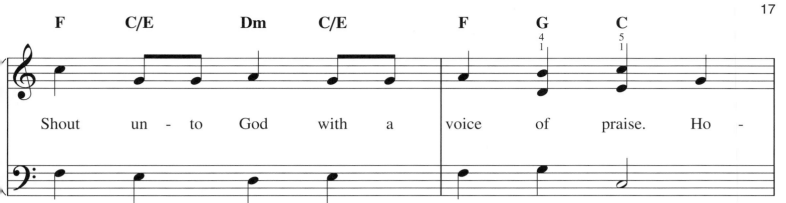

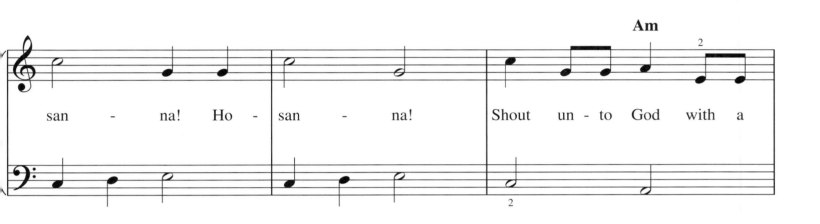

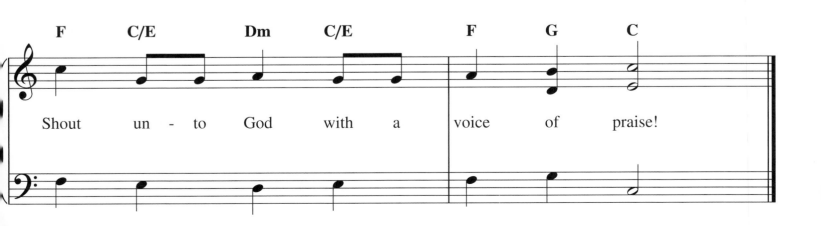

COME INTO HIS PRESENCE

Words and Music by
LYNN BAIRD

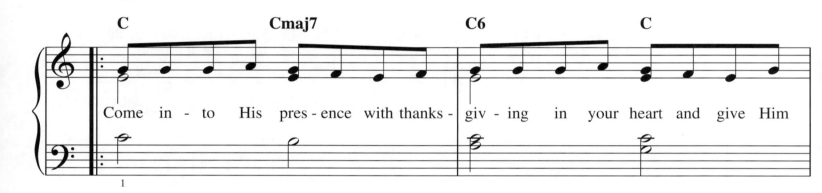

Come in-to His pres-ence with thanks-giv-ing in your heart and give Him

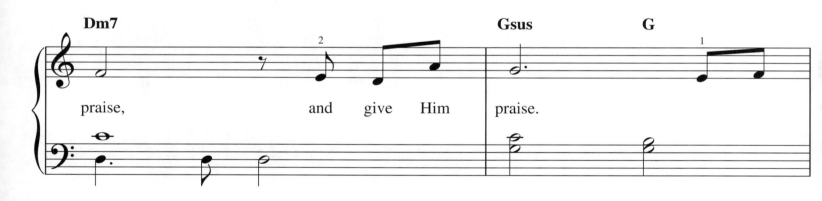

praise,   and give Him praise.

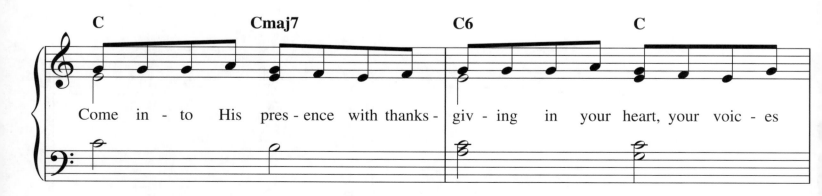

Come in-to His pres-ence with thanks-giv-ing in your heart, your voic-es

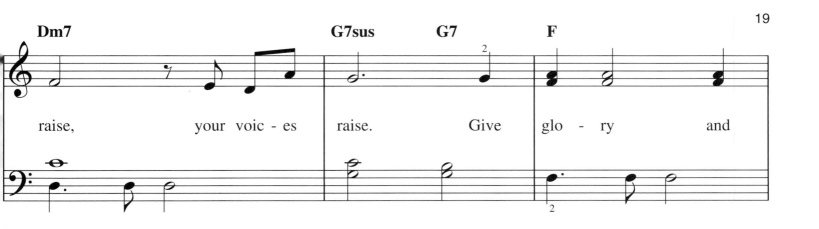

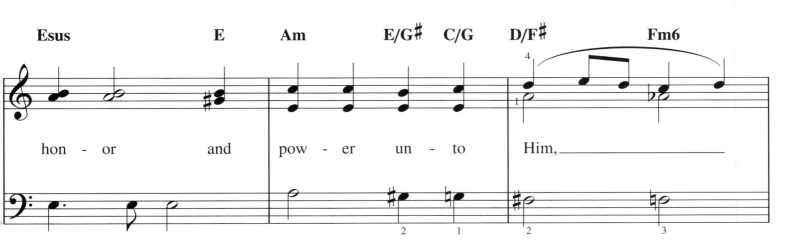

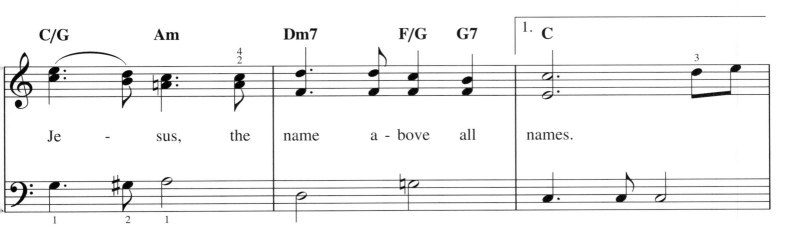

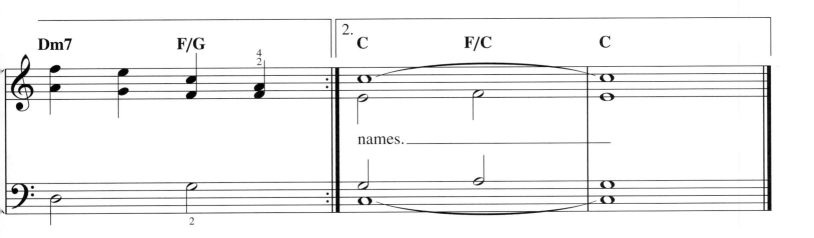

CREATE IN ME A CLEAN HEART

Words and Music by
KEITH GREEN

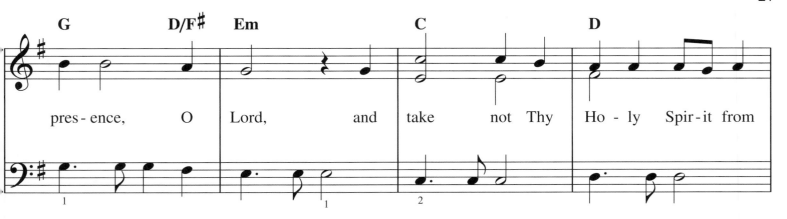

pres - ence, O Lord, and take not Thy Ho - ly Spir - it from

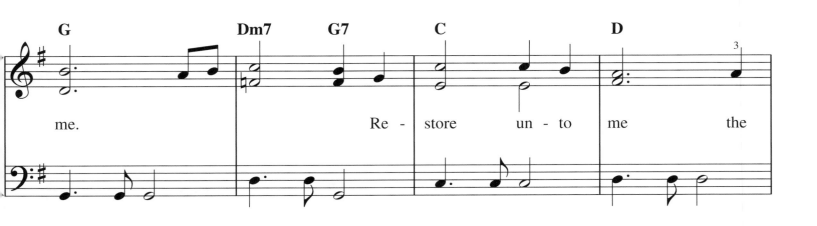

me. Re - store un - to me the

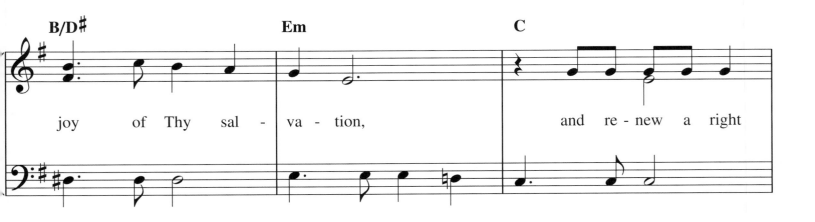

joy of Thy sal - va - tion, and re - new a right

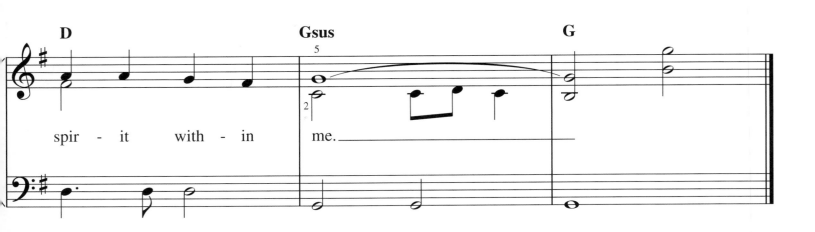

spir - it with - in me.

CREATOR KING

Words and Music by
MARY MacLEAN

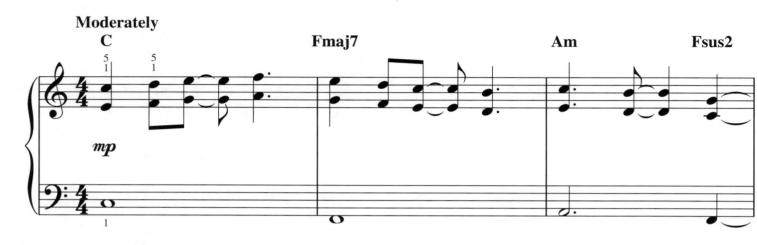

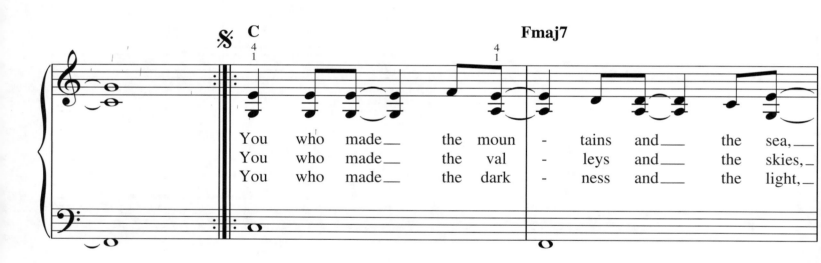

You who made___ the moun - tains and___ the sea,___
You who made___ the val - leys and___ the skies,___
You who made___ the dark - ness and___ the light,___

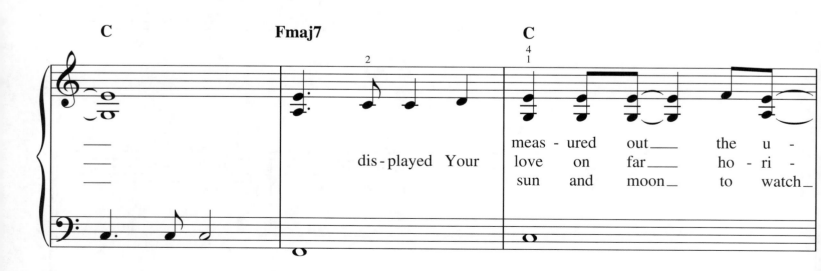

— dis - played Your
— love on far___ ho - ri -
— sun and moon___ to watch___

—
meas - ured out___ the u -
sun and moon___ to watch___

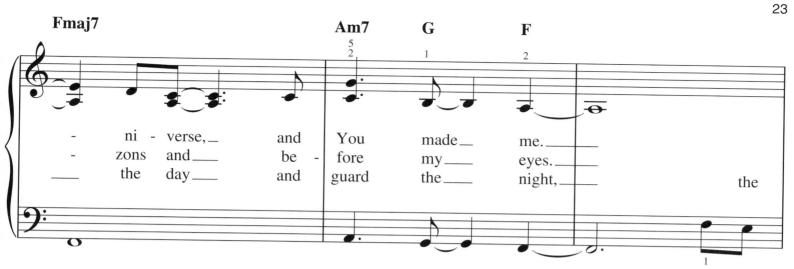

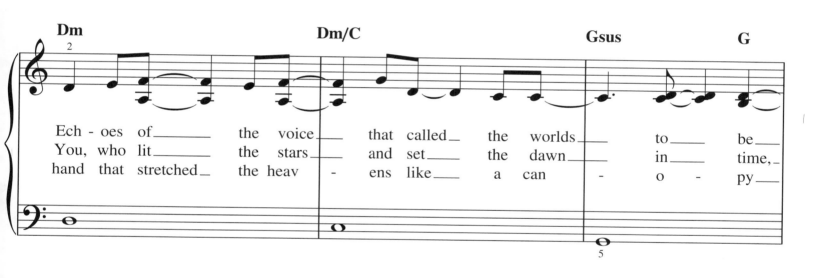

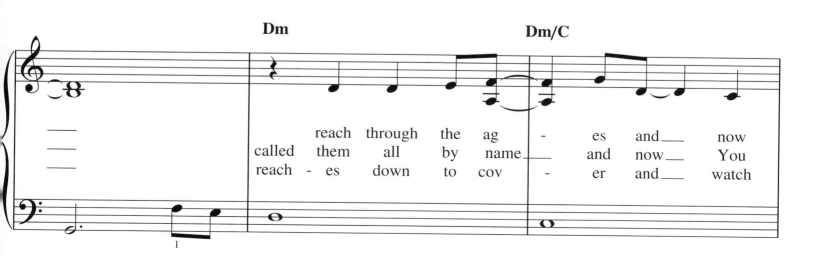

speak to me.
whis - per mine.
o - ver me.

You're
You're
You're

1.
my Cre - a - tor King.

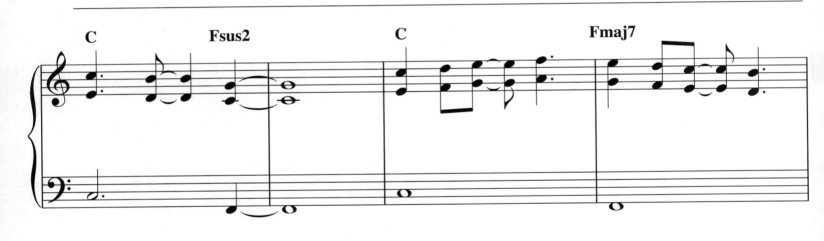

2.
my Cre - a - tor King.

Who am I _____ that You are mind-

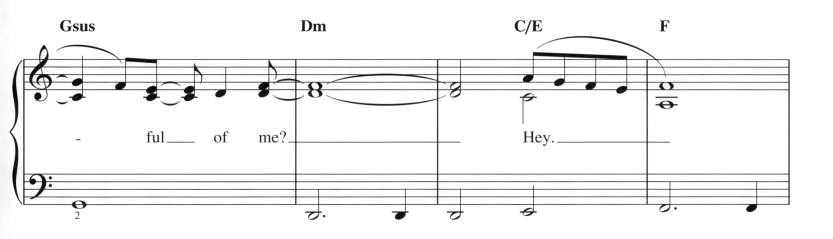

-ful ____ of me? _____ Hey. _____

Who am I _____ that You set ____

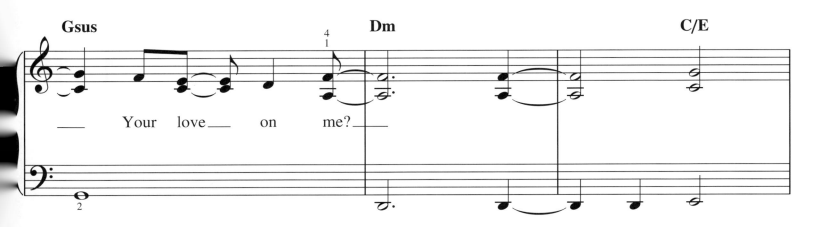

____ Your love ____ on me? ____

26

You're my Cre - a - tor King.

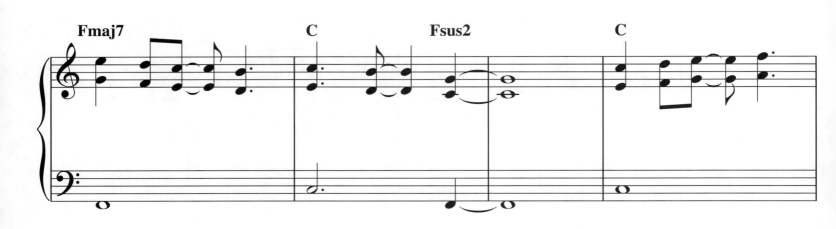

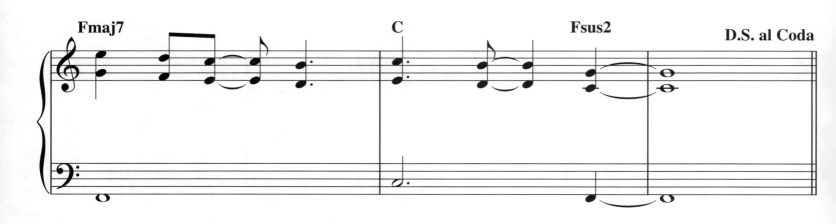

D.S. al Coda

my Cre - a - tor King.

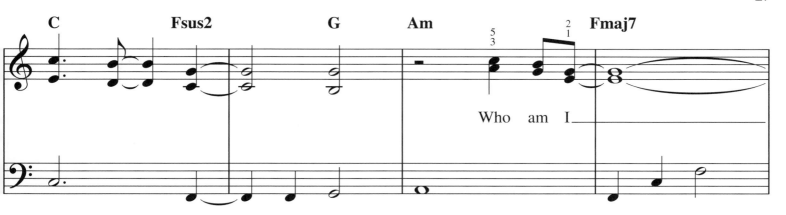

Who am I _____

___ that You are mind - ful__ of me?____

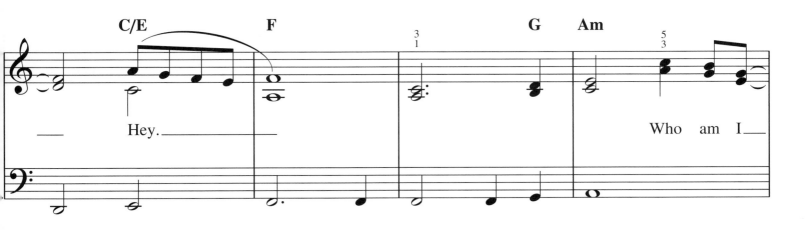

___ Hey._____ Who am I___

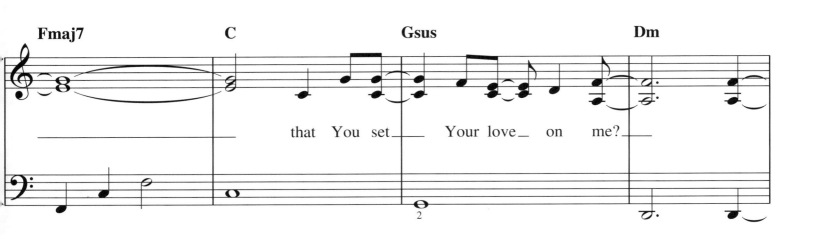

that You set__ Your love_ on me?___

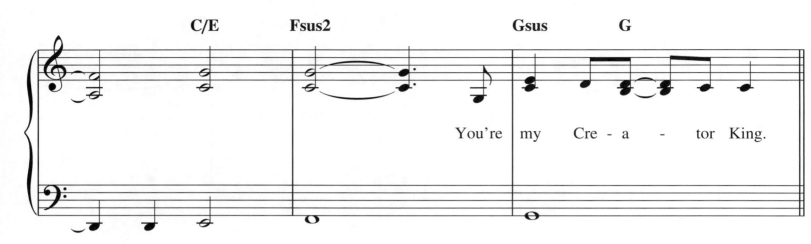

C/E   Fsus2   Gsus   G

You're my Cre - a - tor King.

C   Fmaj7   1.-3.   C   Fsus2

You're

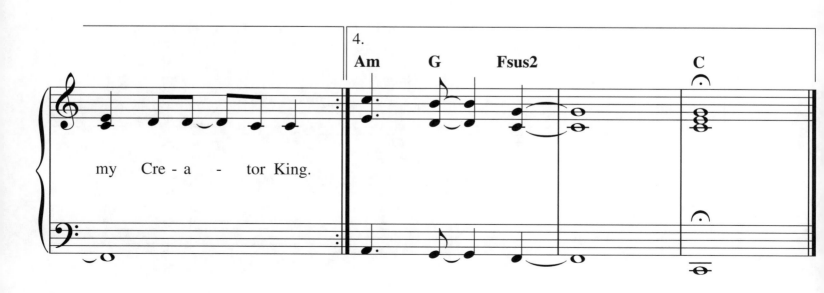

my Cre - a - tor King.

4.
Am   G   Fsus2   C

FRIEND OF GOD

Words and Music by MICHAEL GUNGOR
and ISRAEL HOUGHTON

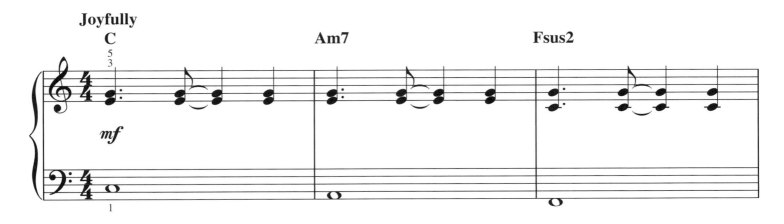

Who am I __ that You __ are mind - ful __ of __

__ me, __ that You hear __ me __

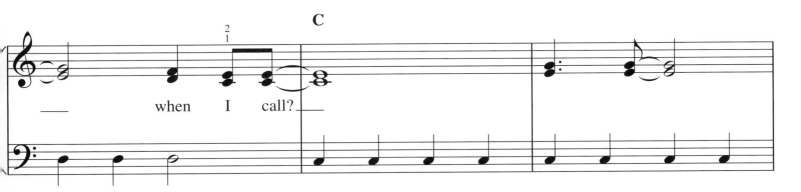

__ when I call? __

Is it true___ that You___ are think - ing___ of___ me?_____

___ How you love___ me,_____ it's a - maz -

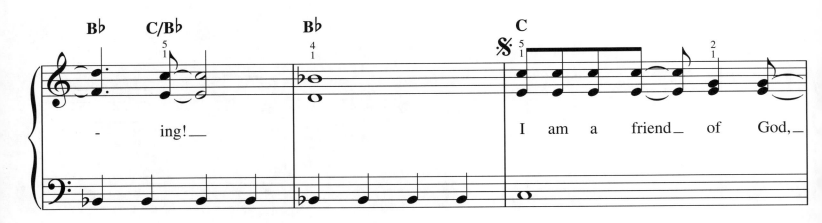

- ing!___ I am a friend___ of God,___

___ I am a friend___ of God,___

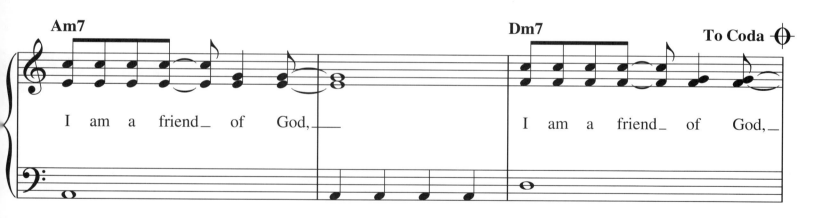

He calls me friend.

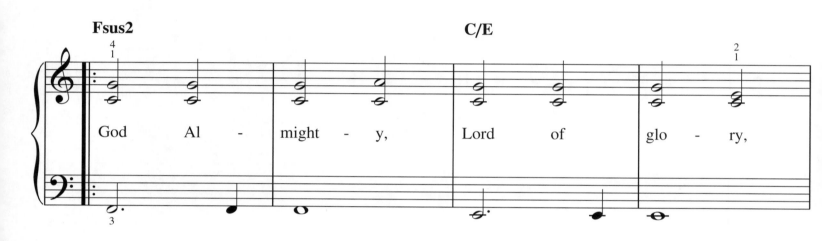

God Al - might - y, Lord of glo - ry,

You have called me friend.

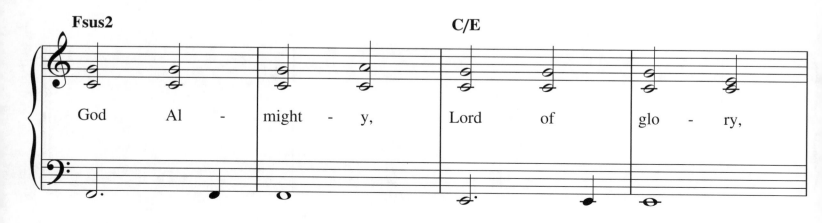

God Al - might - y, Lord of glo - ry,

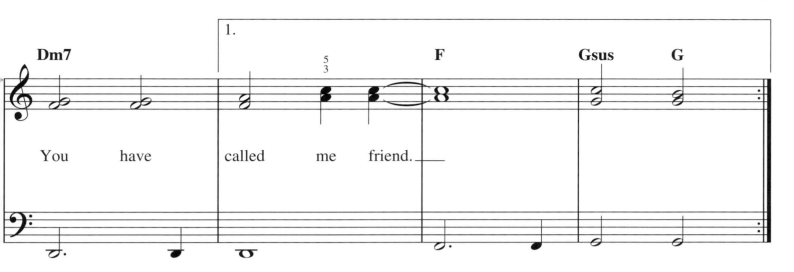

You have called me friend.

called me friend.

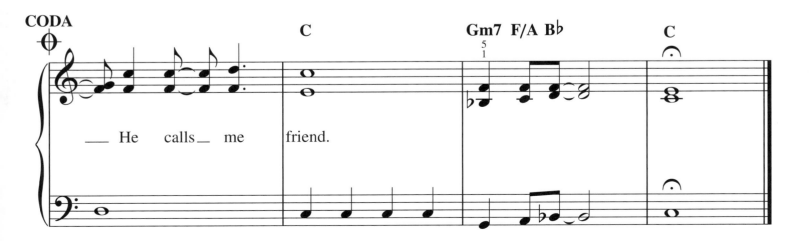

He calls me friend.

DEEP AND WIDE

Traditional

Deep and wide, deep and wide, there's a foun - tain flow-ing deep and

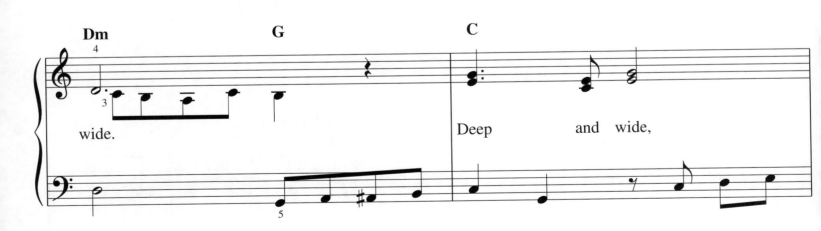

wide. Deep and wide,

DOWN IN MY HEART

Traditional

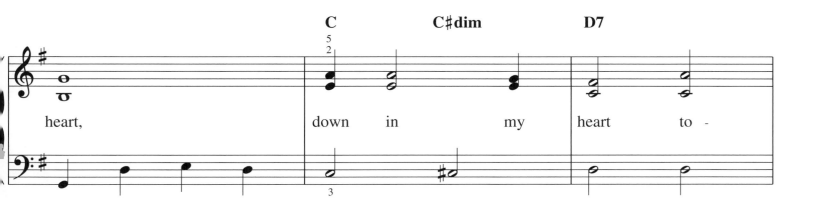

38

down in my heart, down in my

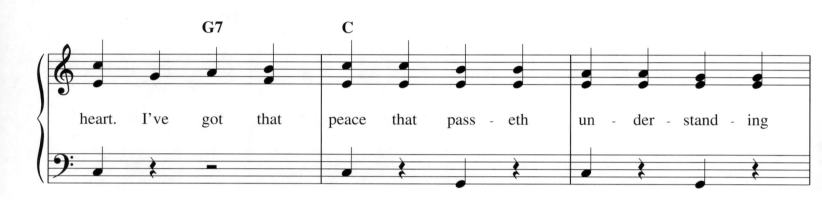

heart. I've got that peace that pass - eth un - der - stand - ing

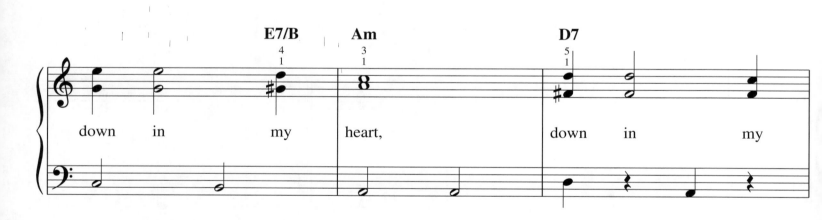

down in my heart, down in my

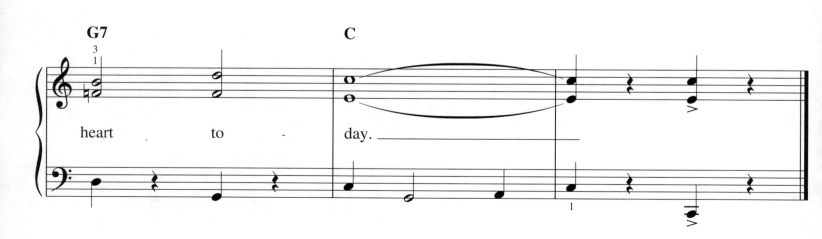

heart to - day. _____

GREAT IS THE LORD

Words and Music by MICHAEL W. SMITH
and DEBORAH D. SMITH

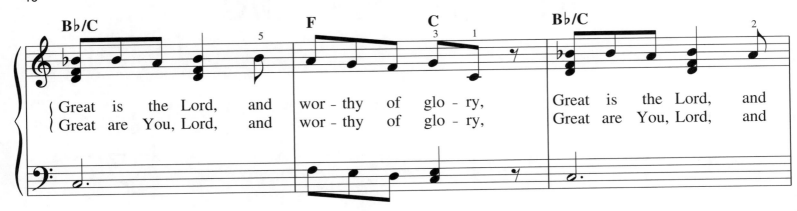

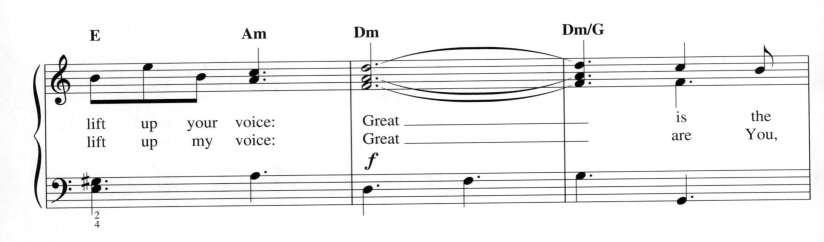

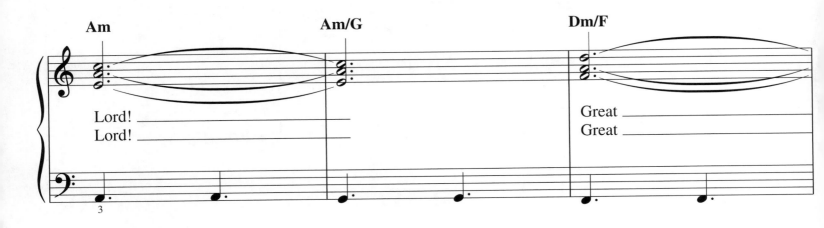

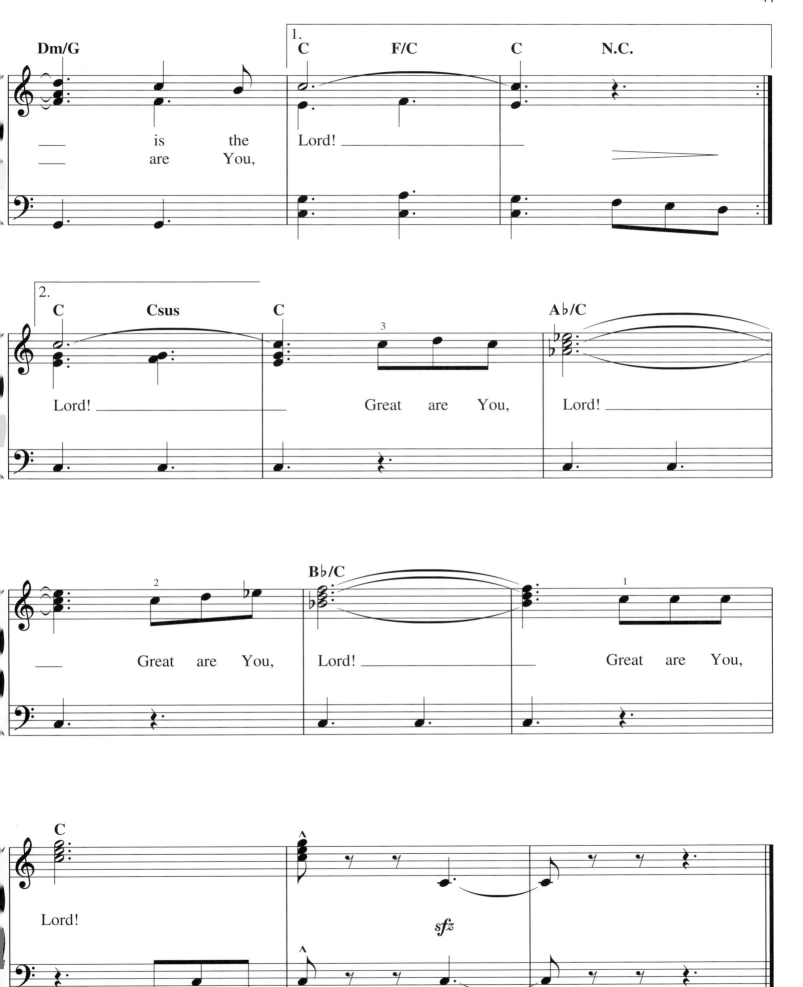

GLORIFY THY NAME

Words and Music by
DONNA ADKINS

43

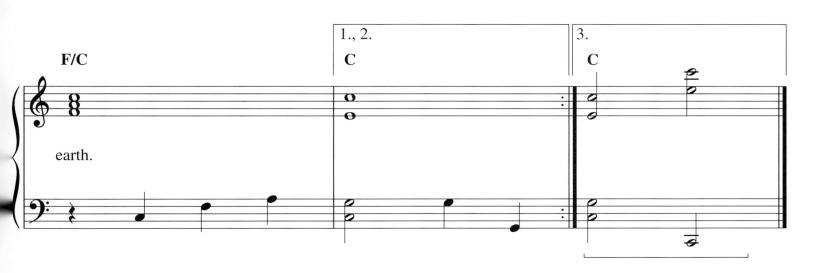

Additional Lyrics

2. Jesus, we love You, we worship and adore You,
Glorify Your Name in all the earth;
Glorify Your Name, glorify Your Name,
Glorify Your Name in all the earth.

3. Spirit, we love You, we worship and adore You,
Glorify Your Name in all the earth;
Glorify Your Name, glorify Your Name,
Glorify Your Name in all the earth.

GOD IS BIGGER

Words by PHIL VISCHER
Music by PHIL VISCHER and KURT HEINECKE

Mysteriously

You were ly - ing in your bed, you were feel - ing kind of sleep - y, but you

could - n't close your eyes be - cause the room was get - ting creep - y! Were those

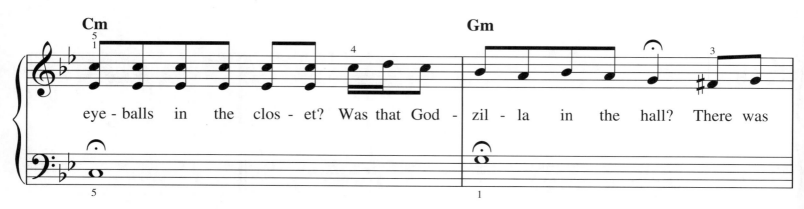

eye - balls in the clos - et? Was that God - zil - la in the hall? There was

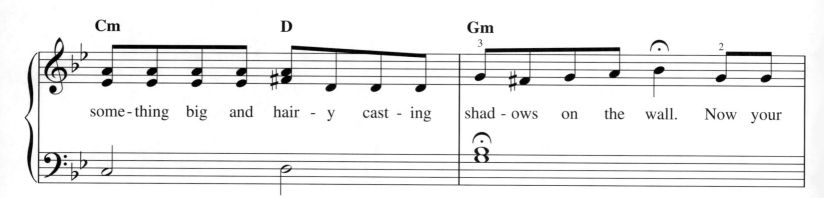

some - thing big and hair - y cast - ing shad - ows on the wall. Now your

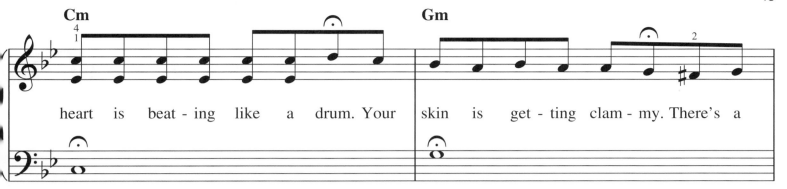

heart is beat - ing like a drum. Your skin is get - ting clam - my. There's a

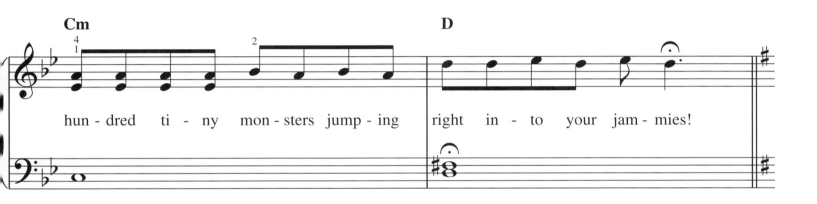

hun - dred ti - ny mon - sters jump - ing right in - to your jam - mies!

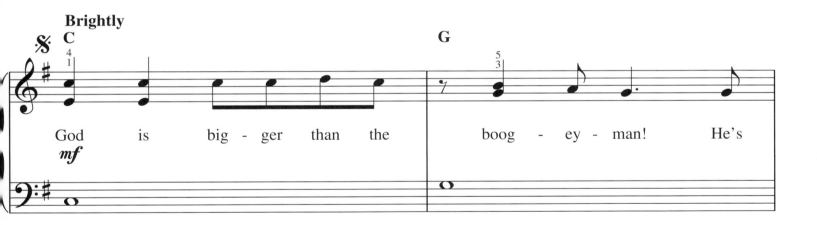

Brightly

God is big - ger than the boog - ey - man! He's

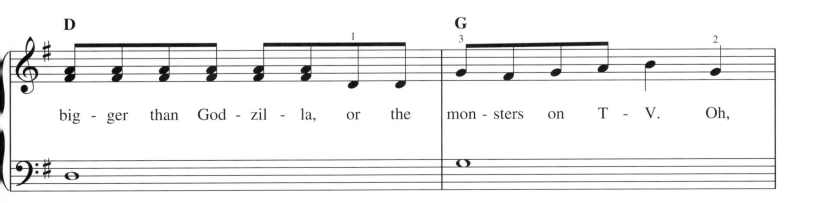

big - ger than God - zil - la, or the mon - sters on T - V. Oh,

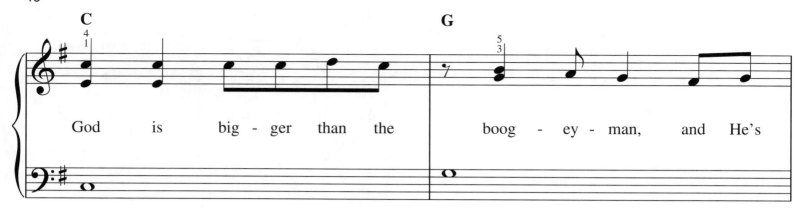

God is big - ger than the boog - ey - man, and He's

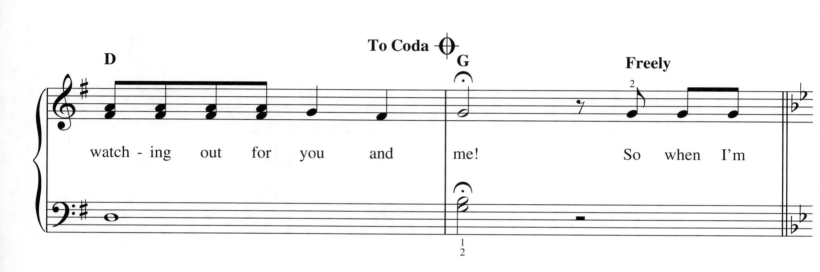

To Coda ⊕

Freely

watch - ing out for you and me! So when I'm

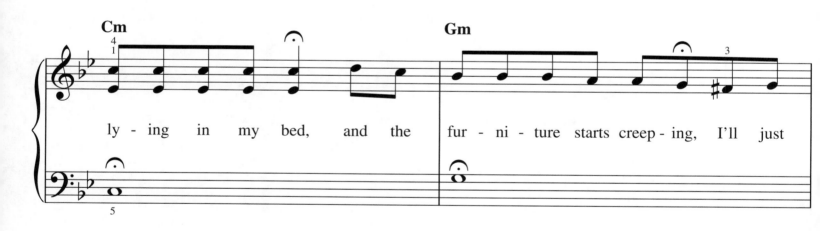

ly - ing in my bed, and the fur - ni - ture starts creep - ing, I'll just

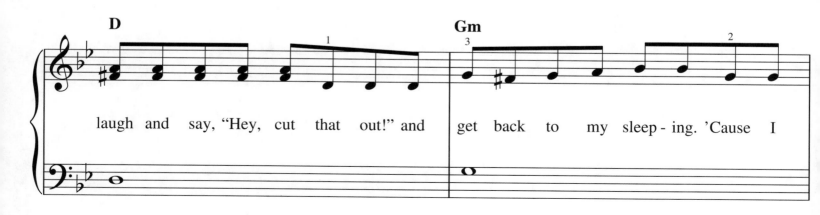

laugh and say, "Hey, cut that out!" and get back to my sleep - ing. 'Cause I

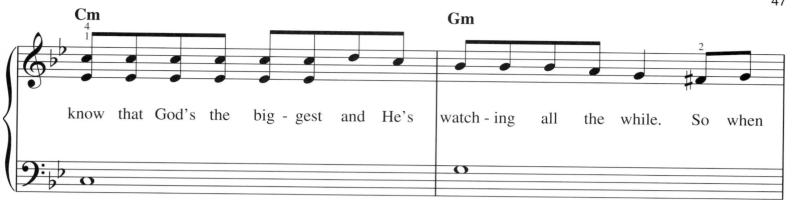

know that God's the big-gest and He's watch-ing all the while. So when

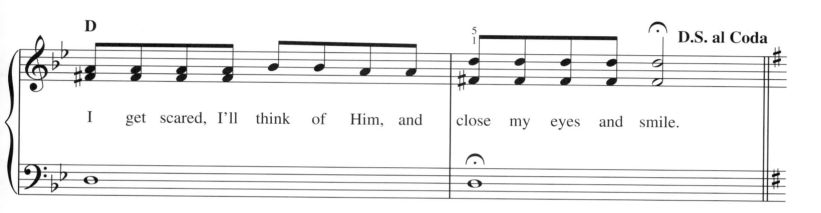

I get scared, I'll think of Him, and close my eyes and smile.

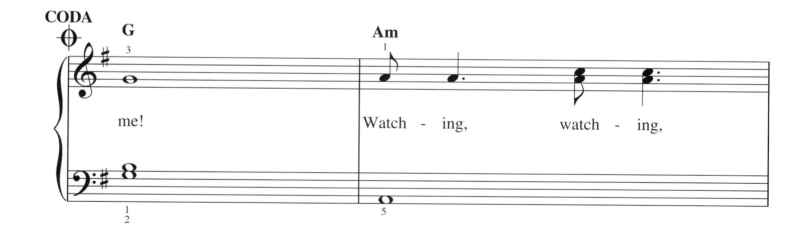

me! Watch-ing, watch-ing,

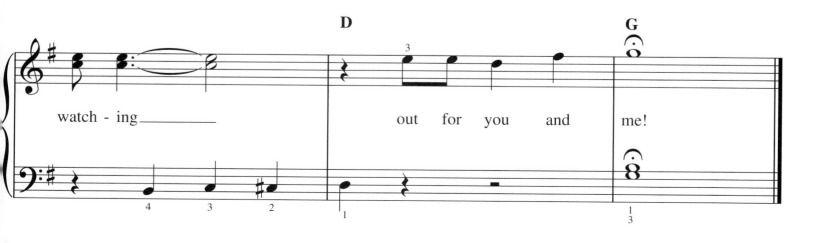

watch-ing_____ out for you and me!

GOD IS SO GOOD

Traditional

50

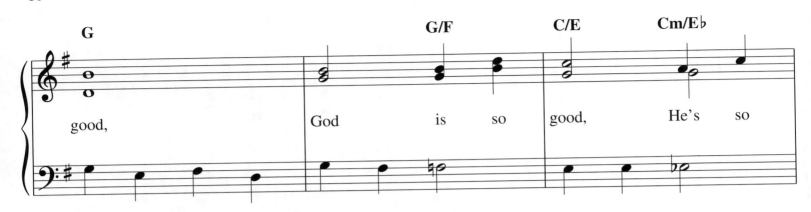

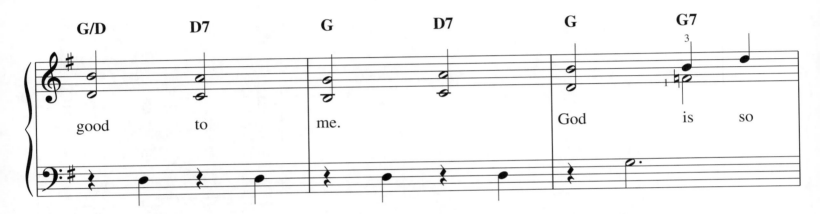

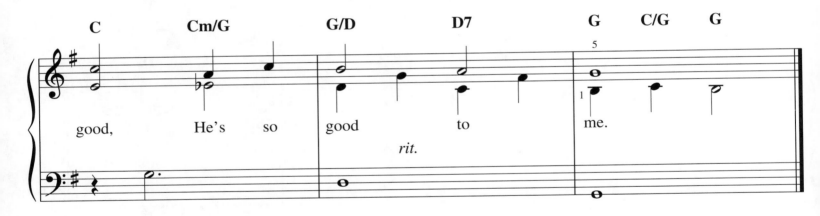

Additional Verses

4. I'll do His will,
   I'll do His will,
   I'll do His will,
   He's so good to me.

5. Jesus is Lord,
   Jesus is Lord,
   Jesus is Lord,
   He's so good to me.

HE IS EXALTED

Words and Music by
TWILA PARIS

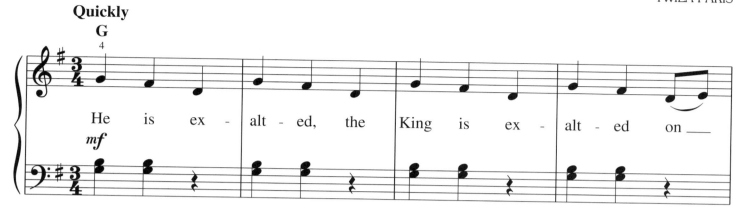

He is ex - alt - ed, the King is ex - alt - ed on ___

high; ___ I will praise Him.

He is ex - alt - ed, for ev - er ex - alt - ed, and

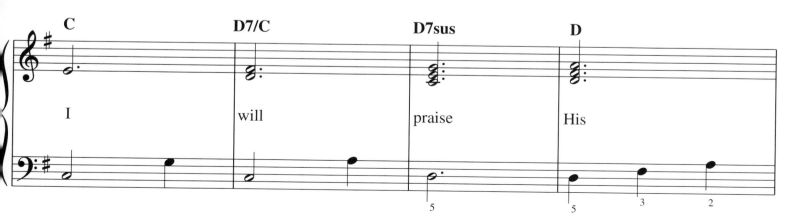

I will praise His

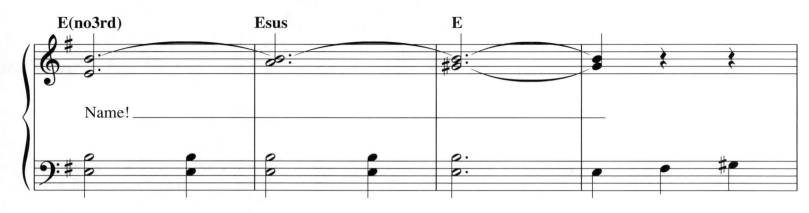

Name!

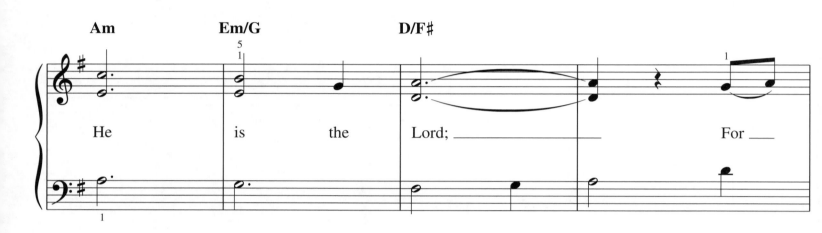

He   is   the   Lord; _____   For ____

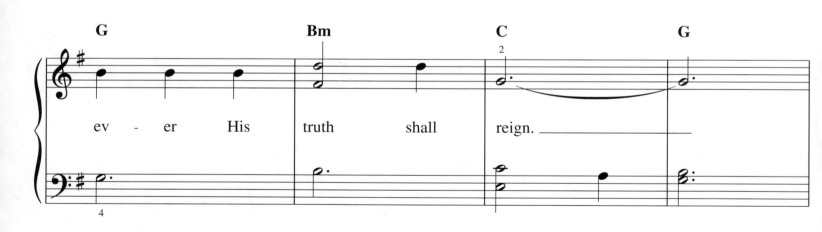

ev - er   His   truth   shall   reign. _____

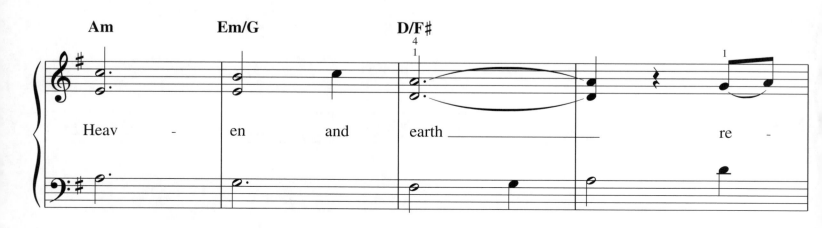

Heav - en   and   earth _____   re -

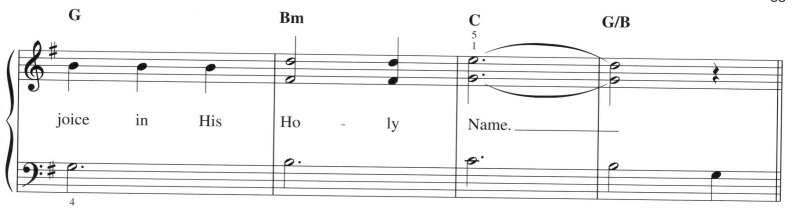

joice in His Ho - ly Name._____

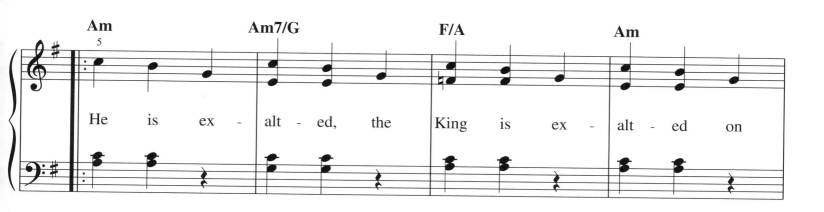

He is ex - alt - ed, the King is ex - alt - ed on

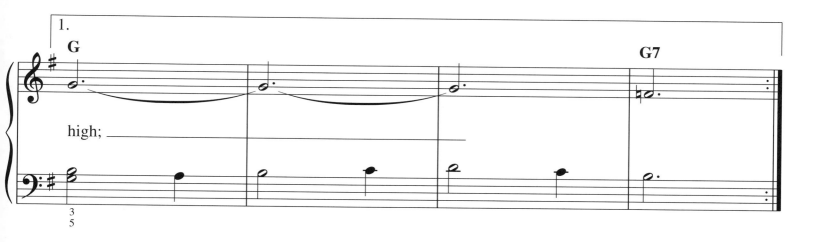

1.

high;_____

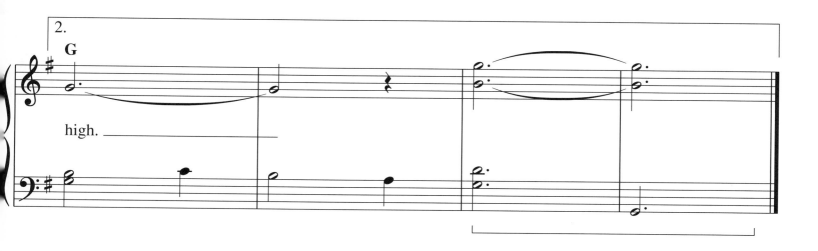

2.

high._____

HALLELU, HALLELUJAH!

Traditional

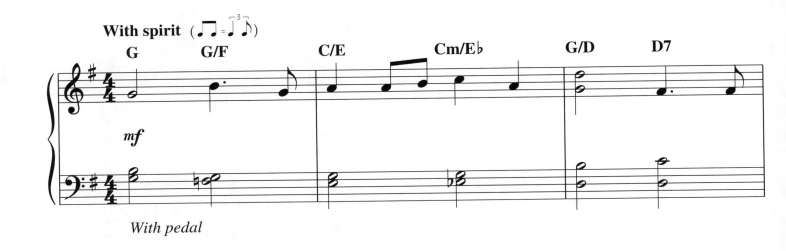

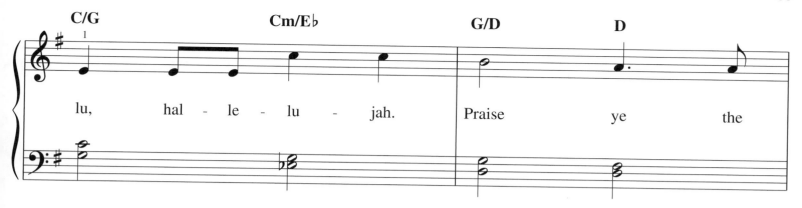

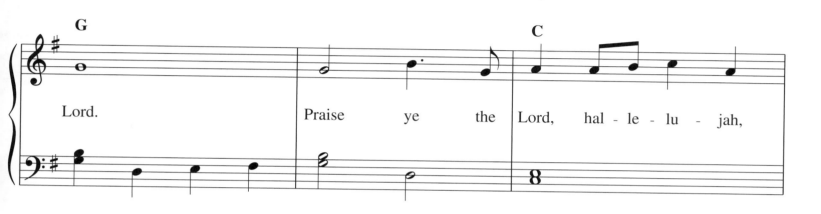

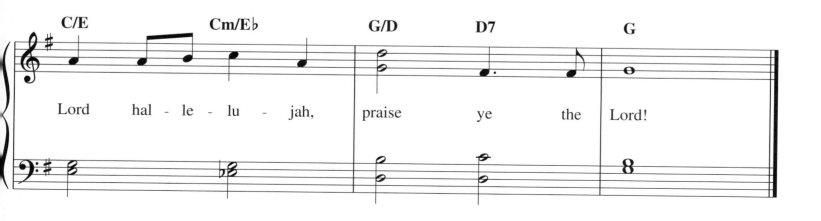

HE IS GOOD

Words and Music by FRANK HERNANDEZ
and JEFF NELSON

Gently flowing

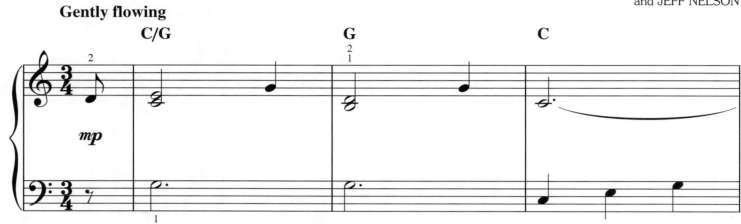

He is good, He is good,_____ His

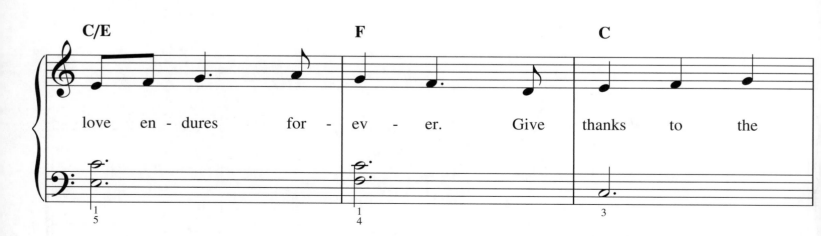

love en - dures for - ev - er. Give thanks to the

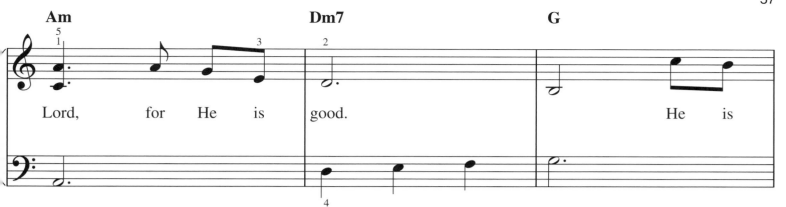

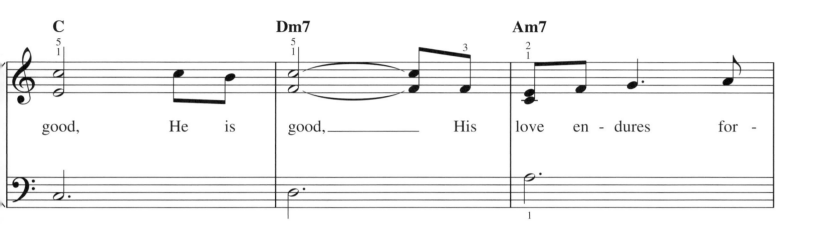

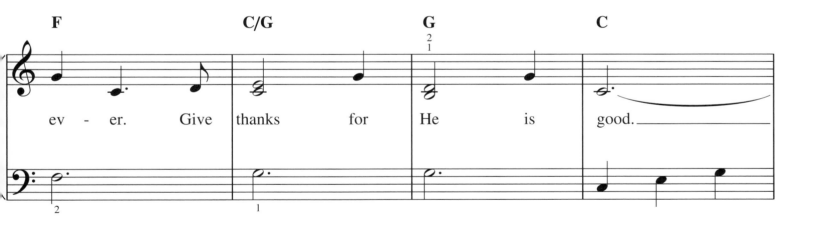

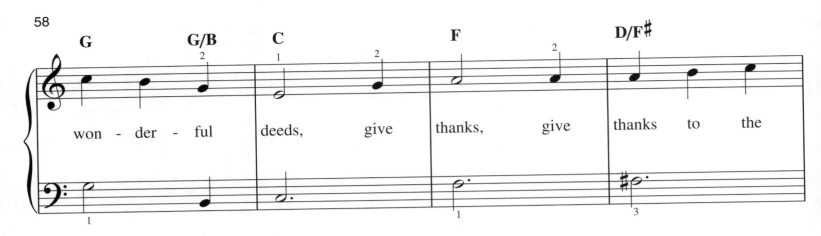

G   **G/B**   **C**   **F**   **D/F♯**

won - der - ful   deeds,   give   thanks,   give   thanks   to   the

G   **C**

Lord._____   He   is   good,   He   is

Dm7   **Am7**   **F**

good,_____   His   love   en - dures   for - ev - er.   Give

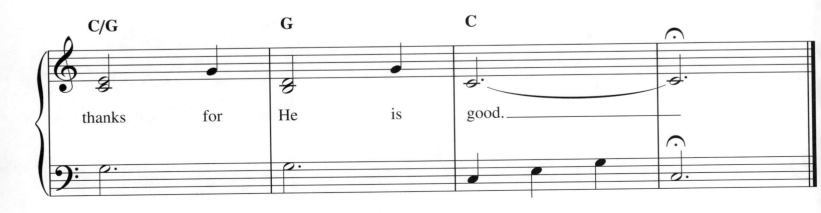

C/G   **G**   **C**

thanks   for   He   is   good._____

HERE I AM TO WORSHIP

Words and Music by
TIM HUGHES

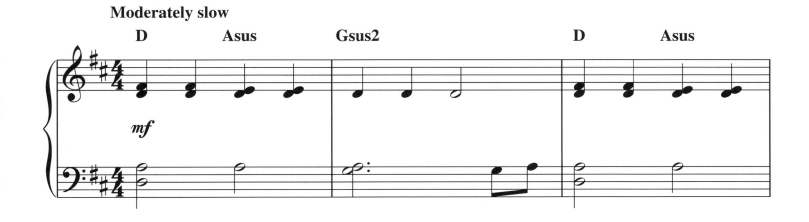

Light of the World, You stepped
King of all days, oh so

down in - to dark - ness,
high - ly ex - alt - ed,

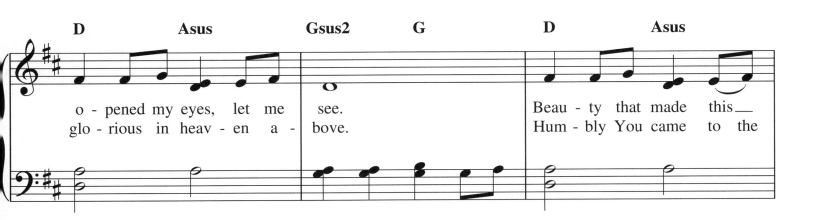

o - pened my eyes, let me see.
glo - rious in heav - en a - bove.

Beau - ty that made this
Hum - bly You came to the

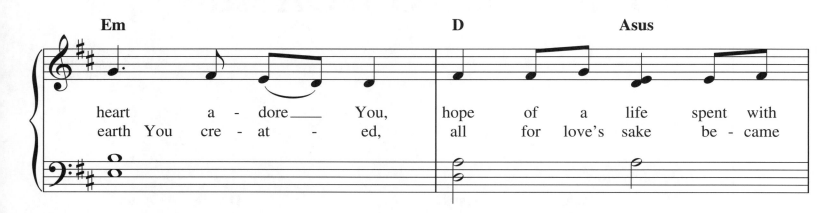

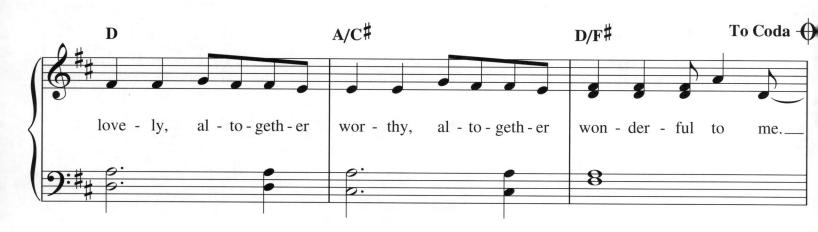

61

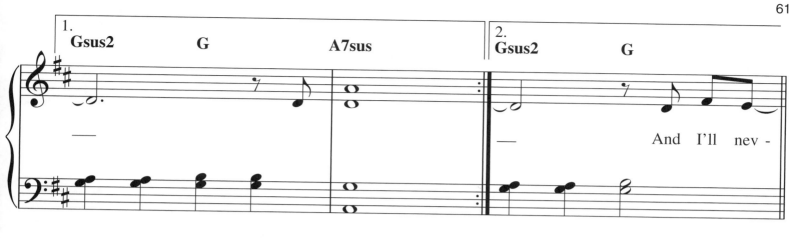

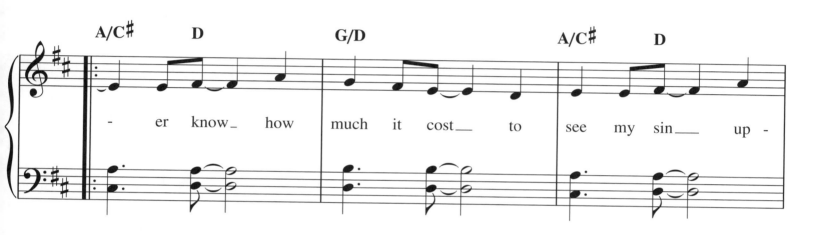

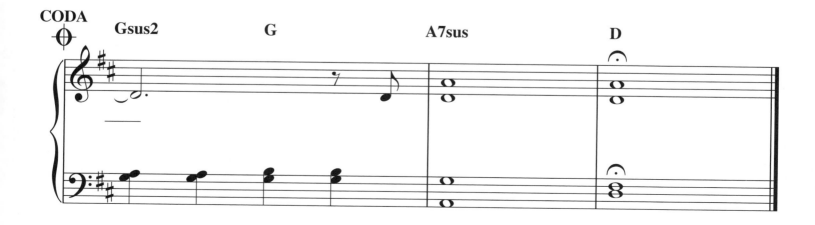

HE'S GOT THE WHOLE WORLD IN HIS HANDS

Traditional Spiritual

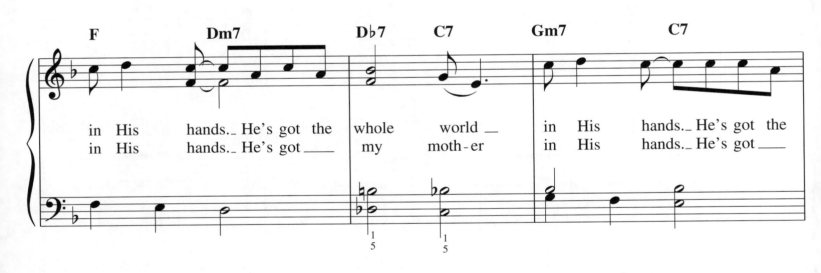

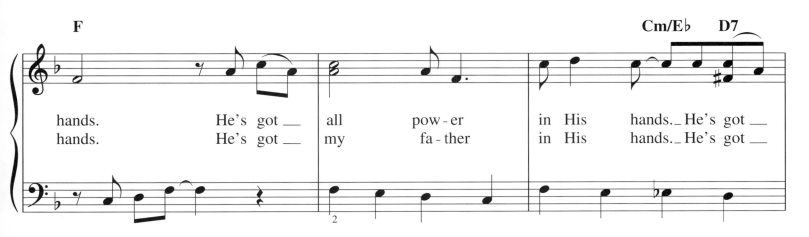

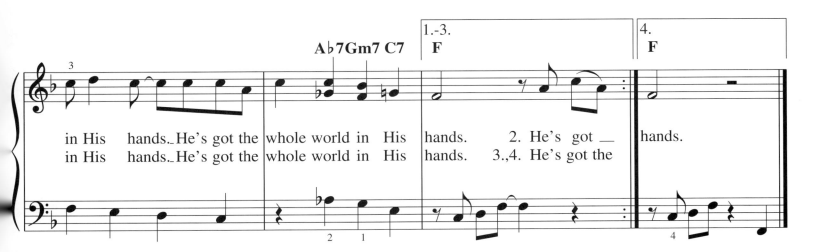

Additional Lyrics

3. He's got the whole church in His hands.
He's got the whole church in His hands.
He's got the whole church in His hands.
He's got the whole world in His hands.

4. He's got the whole world in His hands.
He's got the whole world in His hands.
He's got the whole world in His hands.
He's got the whole world in His hands.

HOW GREAT IS OUR GOD

Words and Music by CHRIS TOMLIN,
JESSE REEVES and ED CASH

With praise

great   is our   God!   Sing with me: How

great   is our   God!   And   all will see how

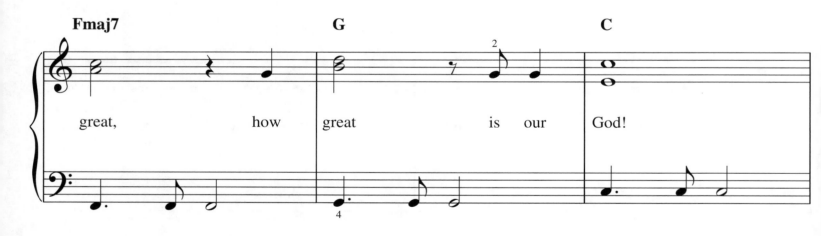

great,   how   great   is our   God!

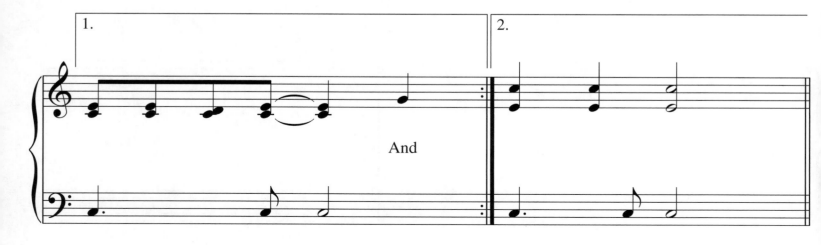

And

Name a - bove___ all names,___

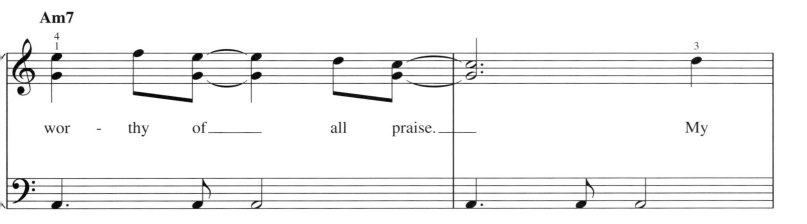

wor - thy of___ all praise.___ My

1.

heart will sing:___ How great is our God!

2.

great is our God!

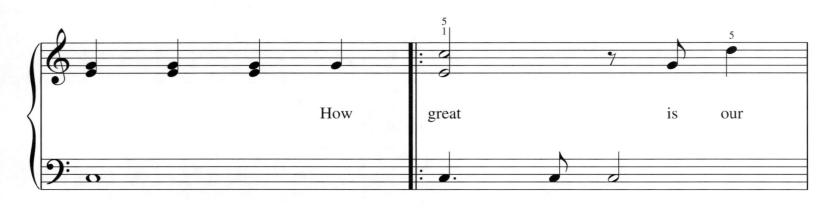

How great is our

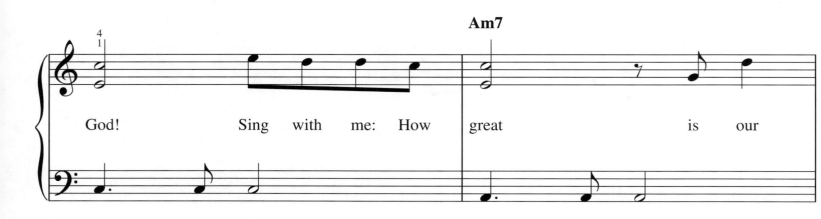

God! Sing with me: How great is our

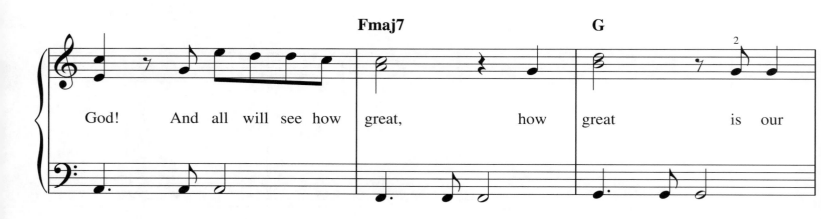

God! And all will see how great, how great is our

God! How God!

HOW MAJESTIC IS YOUR NAME

Words and Music by
MICHAEL W. SMITH

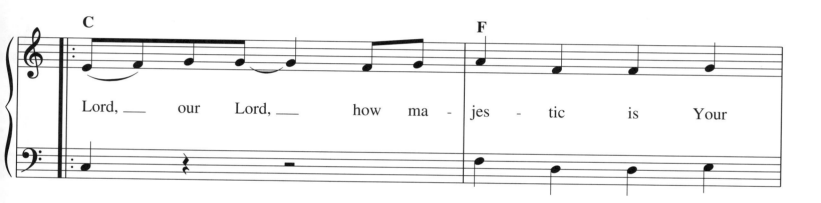

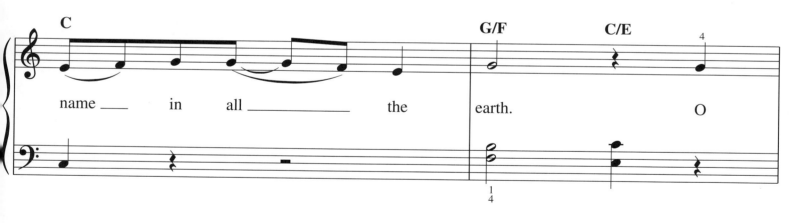

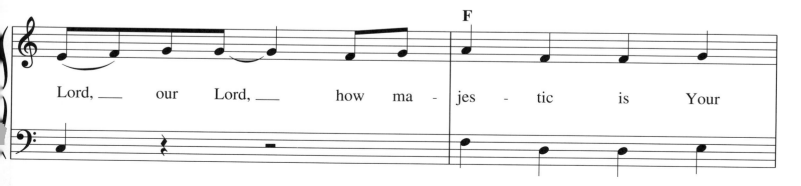

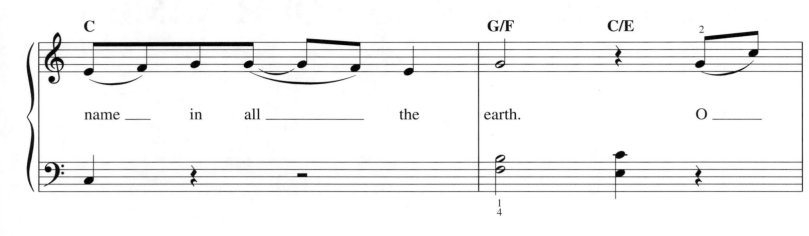

name ___ in all ___ the earth. O ___

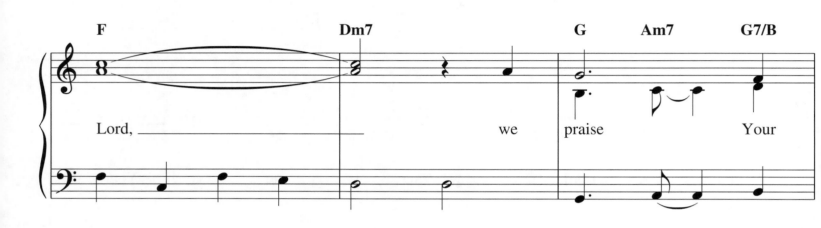

Lord, ___ we praise Your

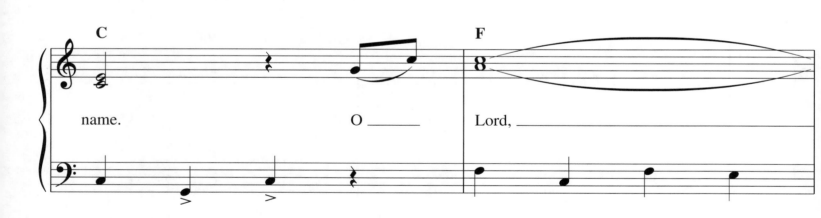

name. O ___ Lord, ___

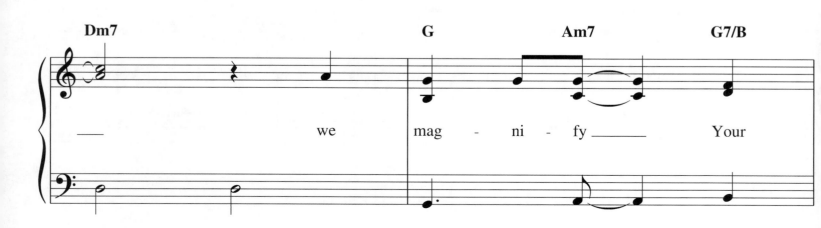

___ we mag - ni - fy ___ Your

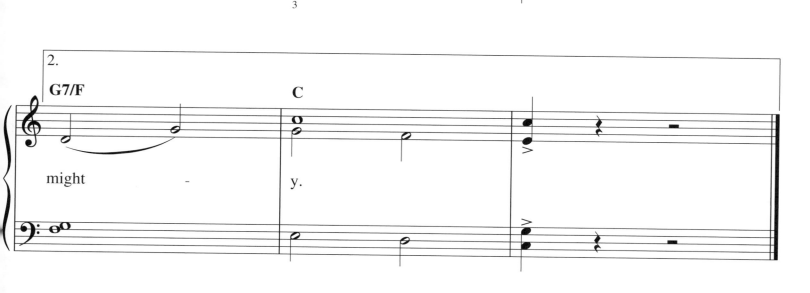

I SING PRAISES

Words and Music by
TERRY MacALMON

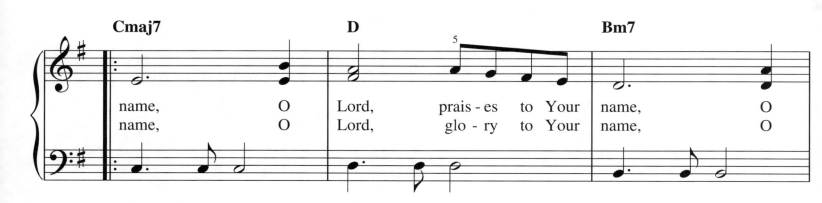

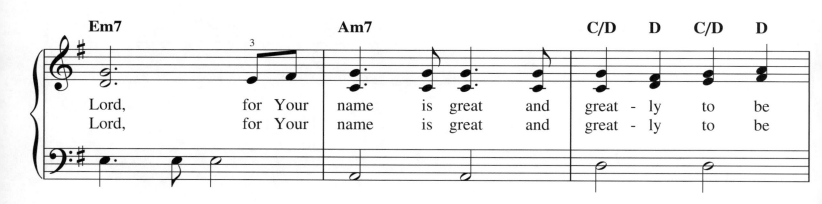

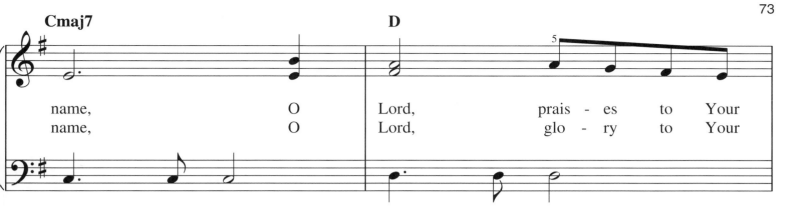

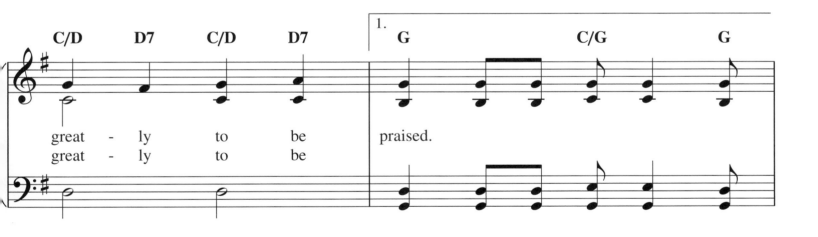

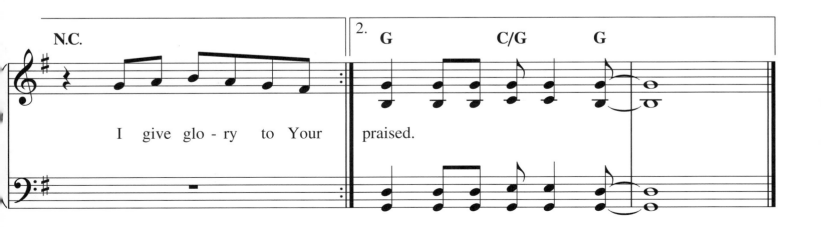

I WILL CALL UPON THE LORD

Words and Music by
MICHAEL O'SHIELDS

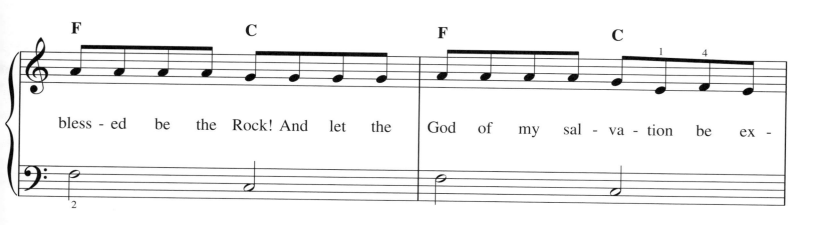

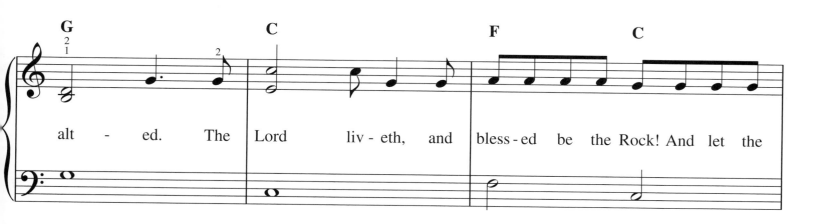

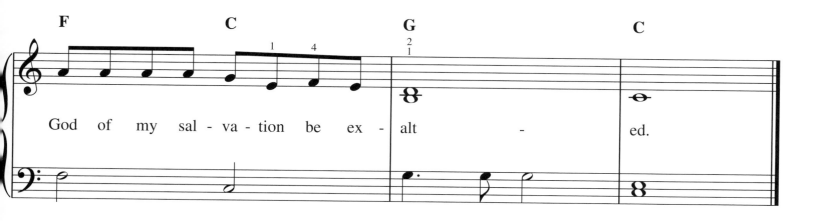

I WILL SING OF THE MERCIES

Words Based on Psalm 89:1
Music by JAMES H. FILLMORE

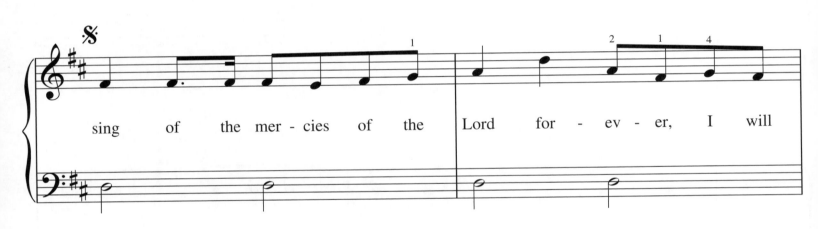

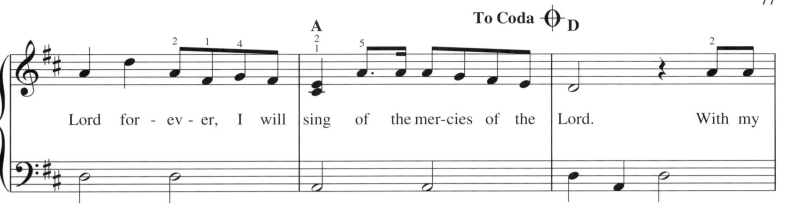

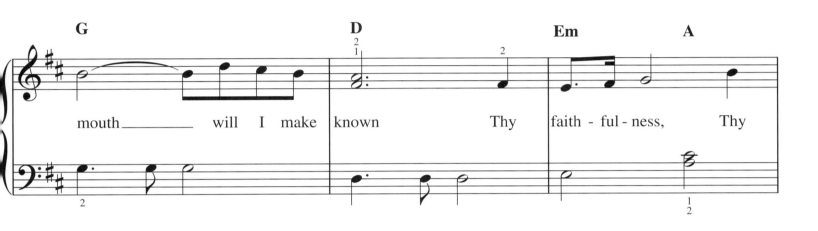

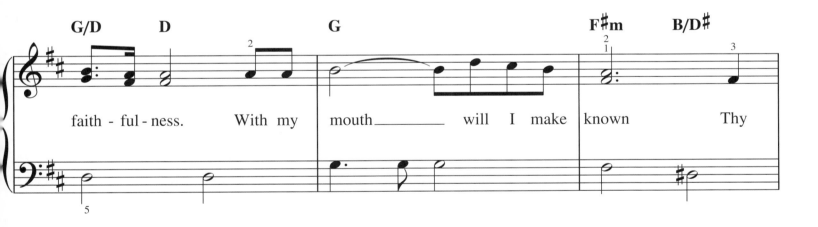

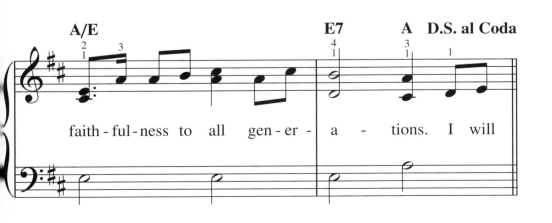

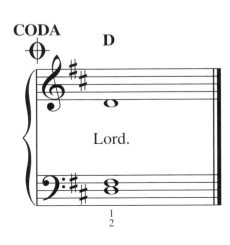

I'VE GOT PEACE LIKE A RIVER

Traditional

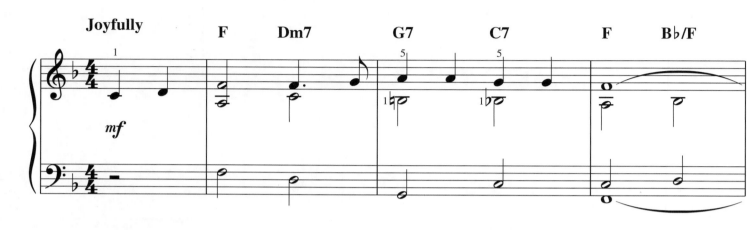

I've got
peace   like   a   riv - er,   I've   got
love   like   a   riv - er,   I've   got
joy   like   a   riv - er,   I've   got

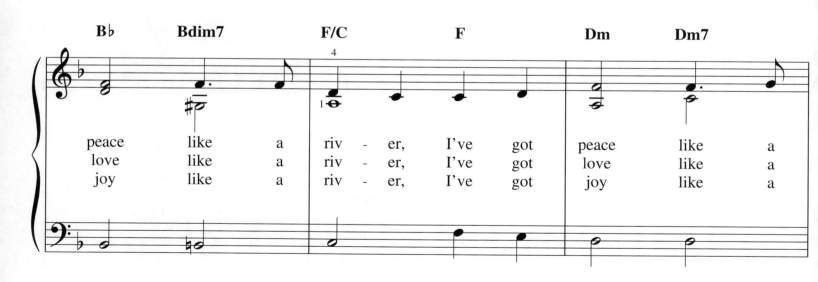

peace   like   a   riv - er,   I've   got   peace   like   a
love   like   a   riv - er,   I've   got   love   like   a
joy   like   a   riv - er,   I've   got   joy   like   a

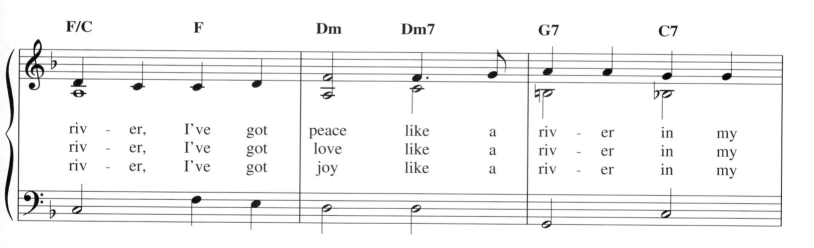
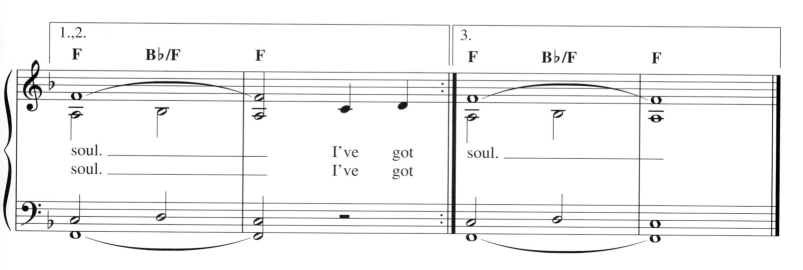

JESUS LOVES ME

Words by ANNA B. WARNER
Music by WILLIAM B. BRADBURY

1. Je - sus loves me! This I know, For the Bi - ble
2. Je - sus loves me! He who died, Heav - en's gate to
3. *(See additional verse)*

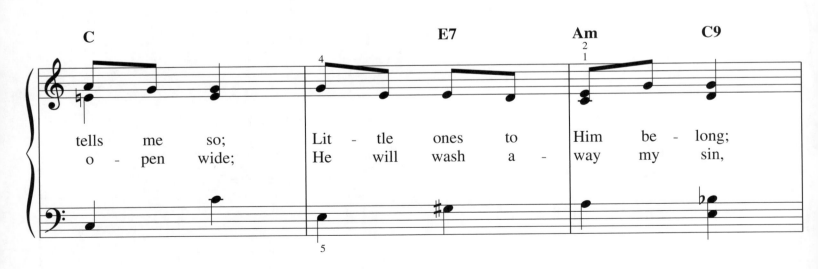

tells me so; Lit - tle ones to Him be - long;
o - pen wide; He will wash a - way my sin,

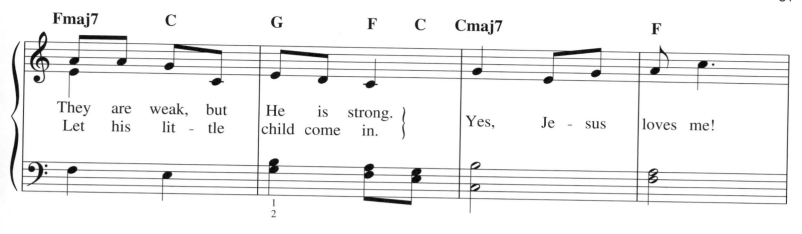

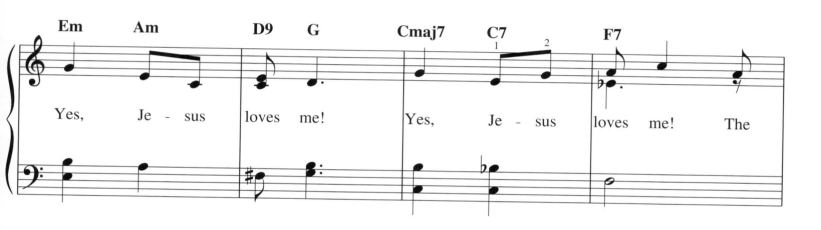

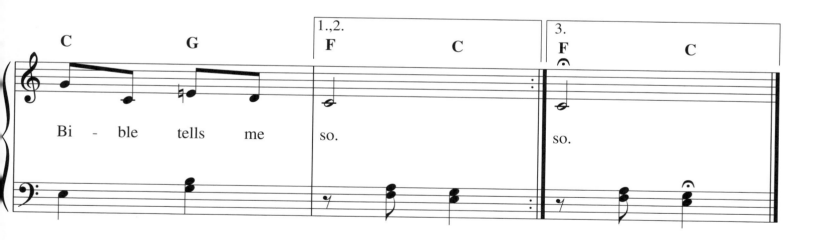

Additional Verse

3. Jesus, take this heart of mine,
   Make it pure and wholly Thine,
   Thou hast bled and died for me;
   I will henceforth live for Thee.
   Yes, Jesus loves me!
   Yes, Jesus loves me!
   Yes, Jesus loves me!
   The Bible tells me so.

JESUS LOVES THE LITTLE CHILDREN

Words by REV. C.H. WOOLSTON
Music by GEORGE F. ROOT

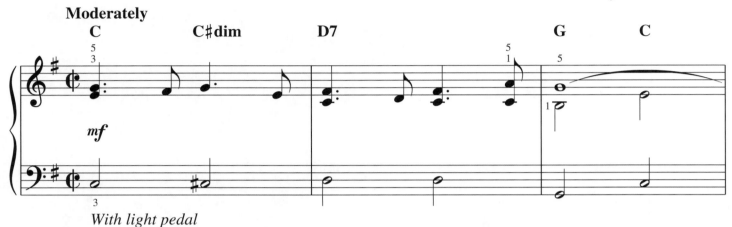

With light pedal

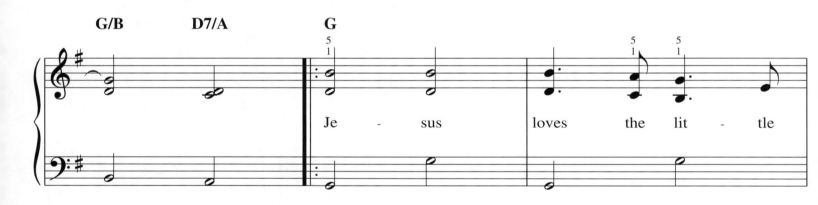

Je - sus loves the lit - tle

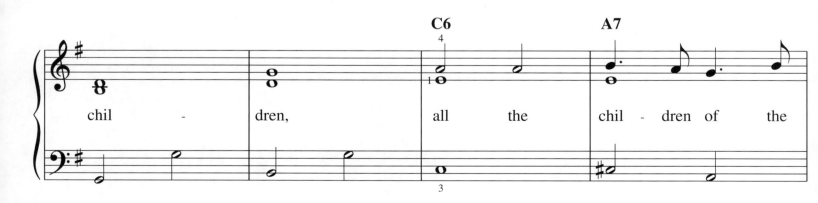

chil - dren, all the chil - dren of the

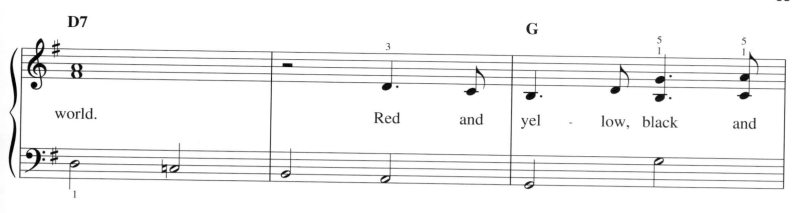

THE JOY OF THE LORD

Text Based on Nehemiah 8:10
Music by ALLIENE G. VALE

The

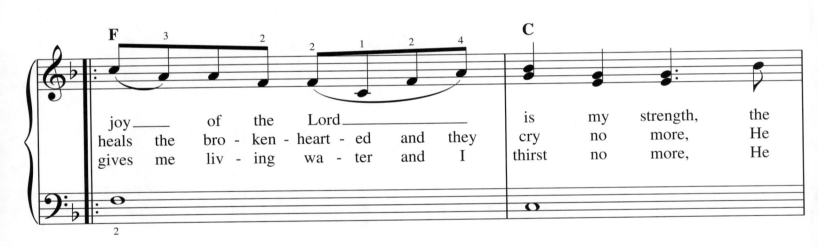

joy		of	the	Lord			is	my	strength,	the
heals	the	bro-	ken-	heart-	ed	and they	cry	no	more,	He
gives	me	liv-	ing	wa-	ter	and I	thirst	no	more,	He

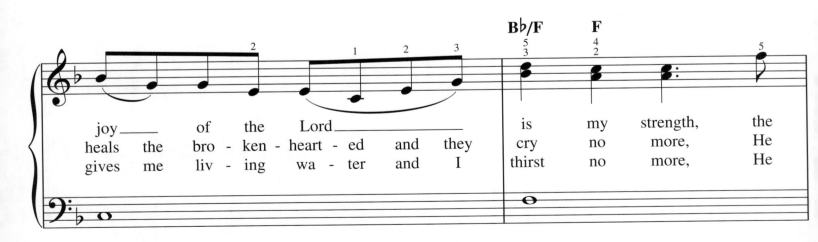

joy		of	the	Lord			is	my	strength,	the
heals	the	bro-	ken-	heart-	ed	and they	cry	no	more,	He
gives	me	liv-	ing	wa-	ter	and I	thirst	no	more,	He

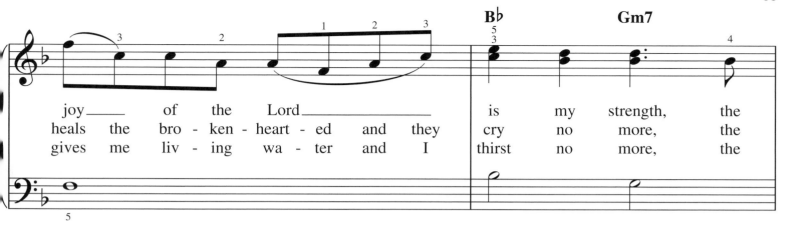

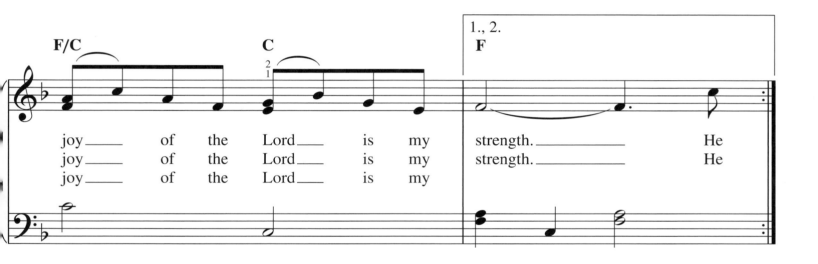

A JOYFUL HEART

Words and Music by
FRANK HERNANDEZ

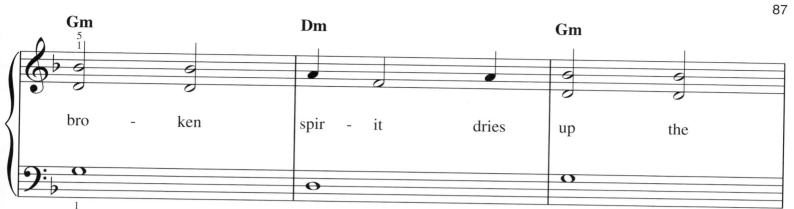

bro - ken spir - it dries up the

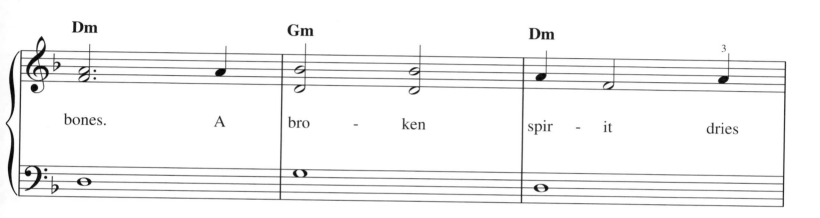

bones. A bro - ken spir - it dries

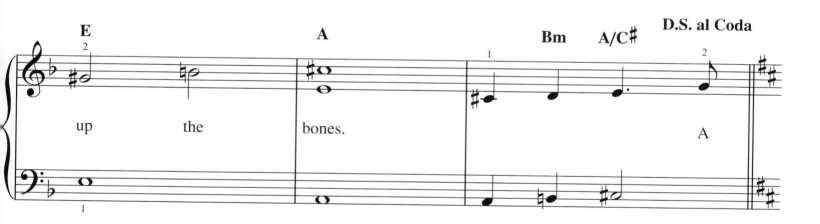

up the bones. A

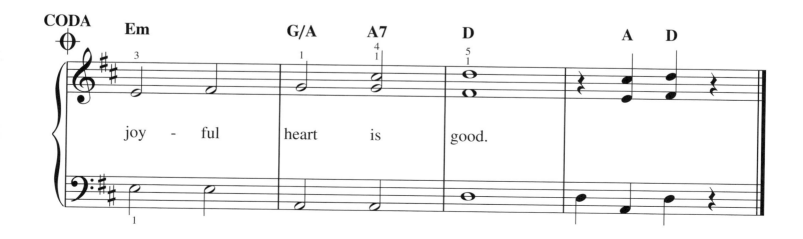

joy - ful heart is good.

KING OF KINGS

Words and Music by SOPHIE CONTY
and NAOMI YAH

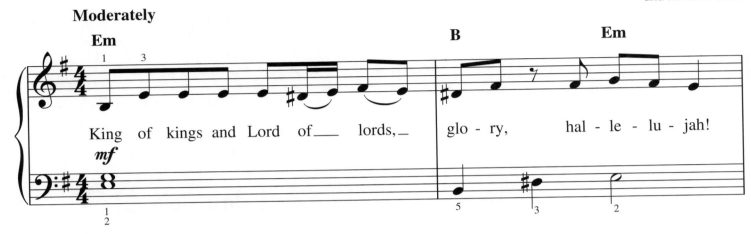

King of kings and Lord of__ lords,__ glo - ry, hal - le - lu - jah!

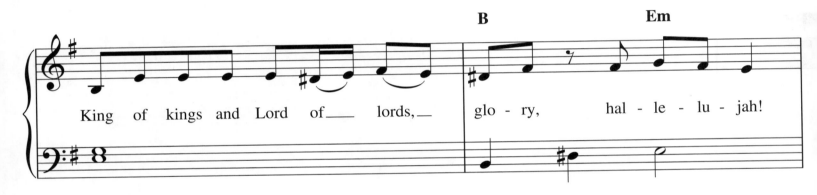

King of kings and Lord of__ lords,__ glo - ry, hal - le - lu - jah!

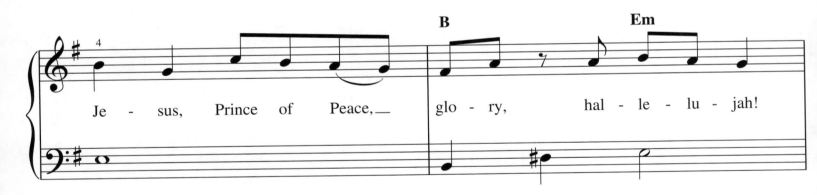

Je - sus, Prince of Peace,__ glo - ry, hal - le - lu - jah!

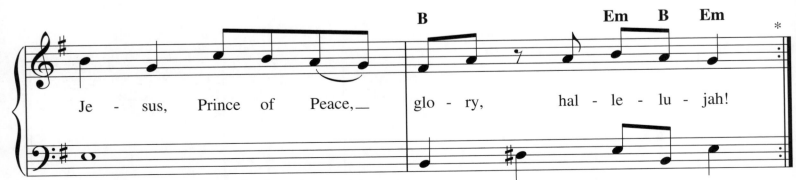

Je - sus, Prince of Peace,__ glo - ry, hal - le - lu - jah!

Repeat several times, increasing the tempo each time.

MORE PRECIOUS THAN SILVER

Words and Music by
LYNN DeSHAZO

Warmly, with expression

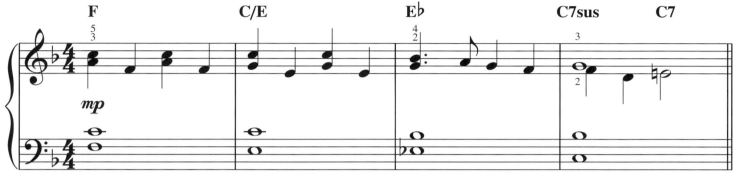

With pedal

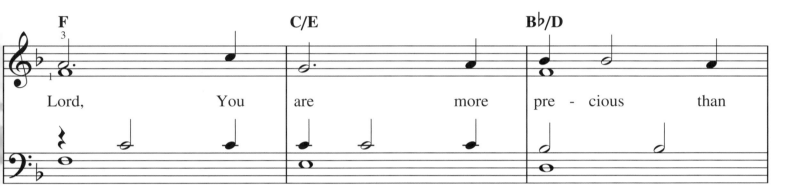

Lord, You are more pre - cious than

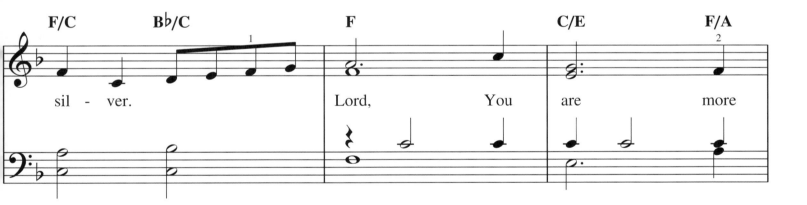

sil - ver. Lord, You are more

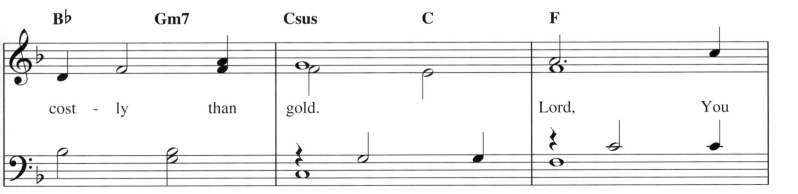

cost - ly than gold. Lord, You

90

are more beau - ti - ful____ than dia - monds, and

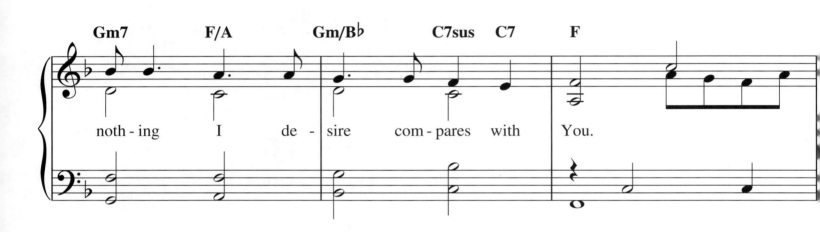

noth - ing I de - sire com - pares with You.

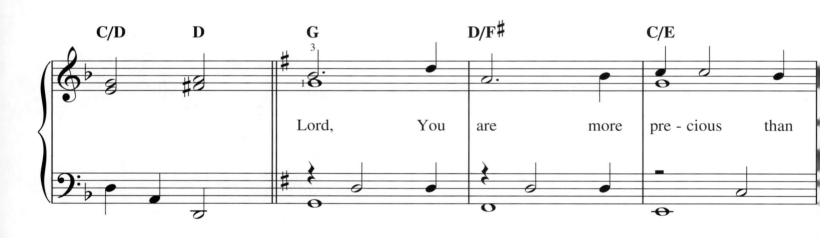

Lord, You are more pre - cious than

sil - ver. Lord, You are more

C   Am7   Dsus   D   G   D/F♯

cost - ly   than   gold.   Lord,   You   are   more

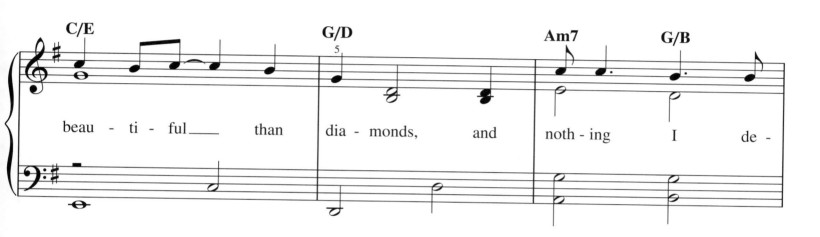

C/E   G/D   Am7   G/B

beau - ti - ful___ than   dia - monds,   and   noth - ing   I   de -

Am7/C   D7sus   D7   Em   C♯m7♭5

sire   com-pares   with   You.

Am7   G/B   Am/C   D7sus   D7   G   C/G   G

Noth - ing   I   de - sire   com-pares   with   You.

rit.

LORD, I WANT TO BE A CHRISTIAN

Traditional Spiritual

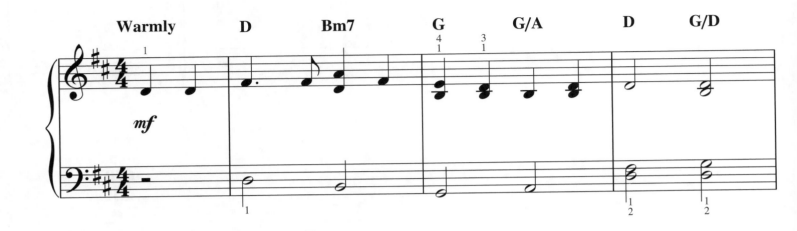

Lord, I want to be

{ a Chris - tian }
{ more lov - ing }
{ more ho - ly }
{ like Je - sus }

in my

heart, in my heart.___ Lord, I want to be

{ a
{ more
{ more
{ like

LOVE YOUR NEIGHBOR

Words and Music by
PHIL VISCHER

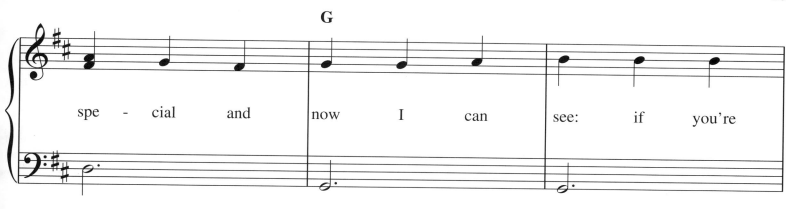

G

spe - cial and now I can see: if you're

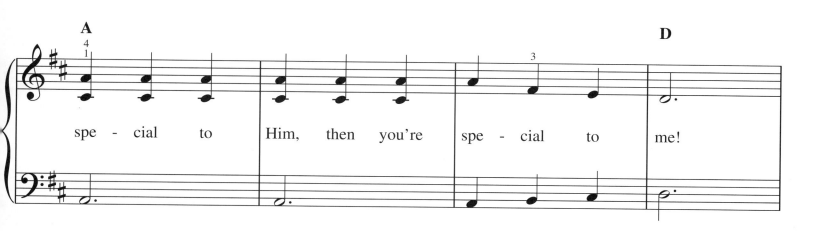

A   D

spe - cial to Him, then you're spe - cial to me!

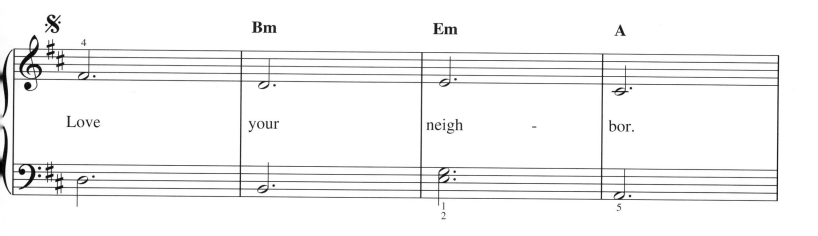

Bm   Em   A

Love your neigh - bor.

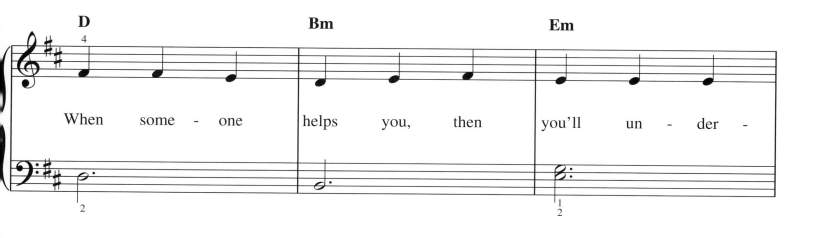

D   Bm   Em

When some - one helps you, then you'll un - der -

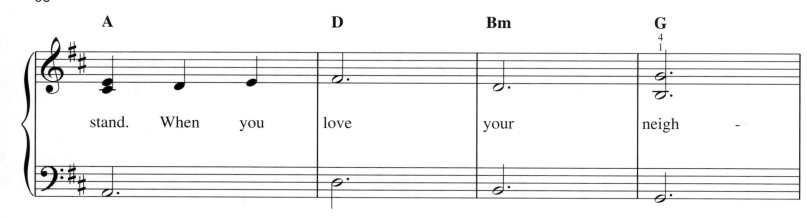

A   D   Bm   G

stand.   When   you   love   your   neigh -

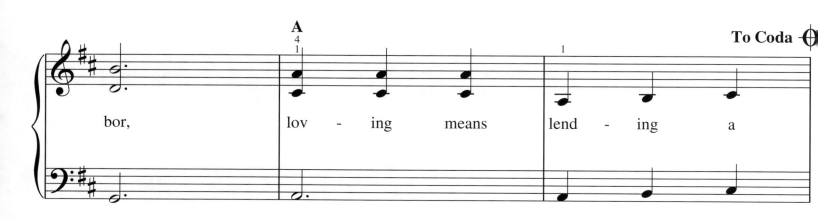

A   To Coda

bor,   lov - ing   means   lend - ing   a

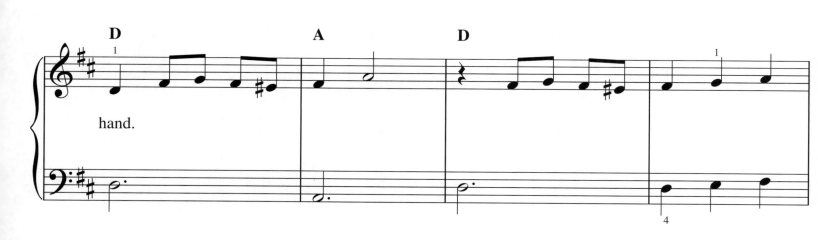

D   A   D

hand.

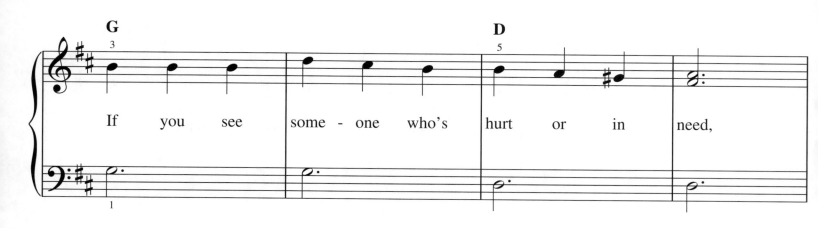

G   D

If   you   see   some - one   who's   hurt   or   in   need,

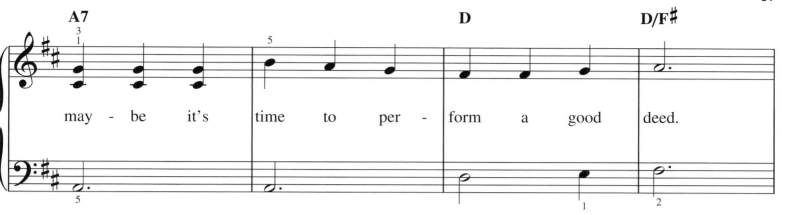

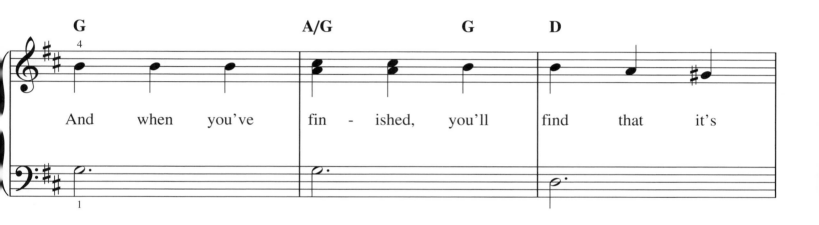

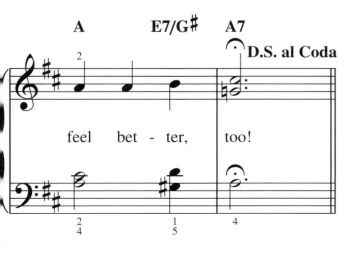
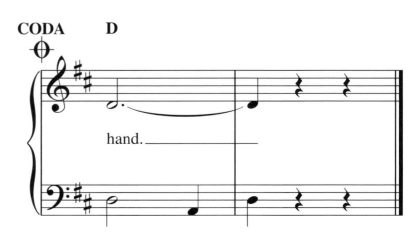

MY GOD IS SO GREAT, SO STRONG AND SO MIGHTY

Traditional

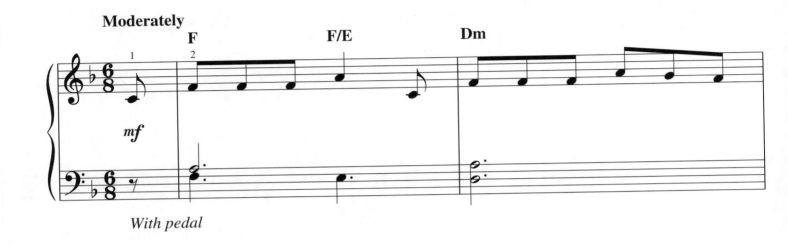

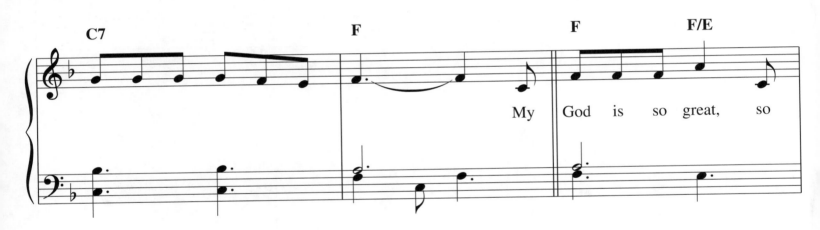

God is so great, so strong and so might-y! There's noth-ing my God can-not

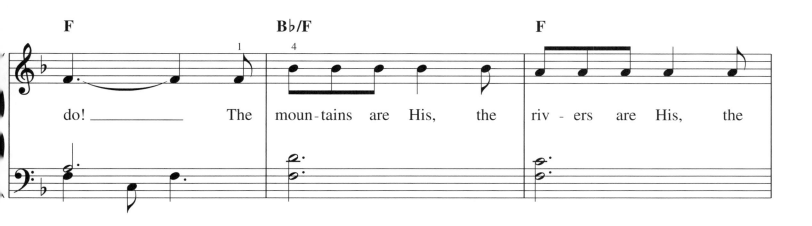

do! _____ The moun-tains are His, the riv-ers are His, the

stars are His hand-i-work, too. _____ My God is so great, so

strong and so might-y! There's noth-ing my God can-not do!

OH, BE CAREFUL

Traditional

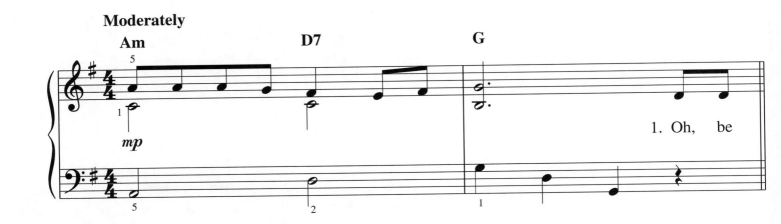

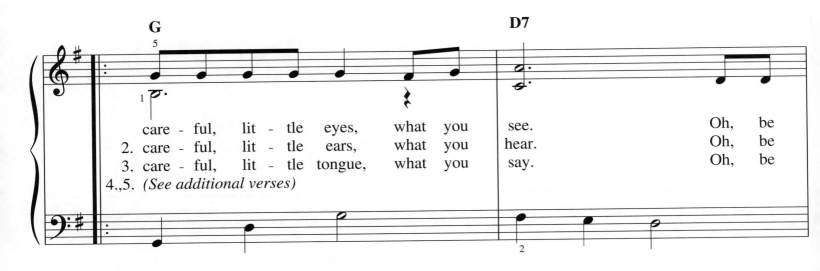

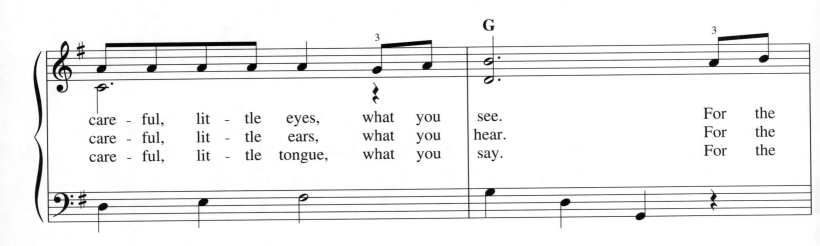

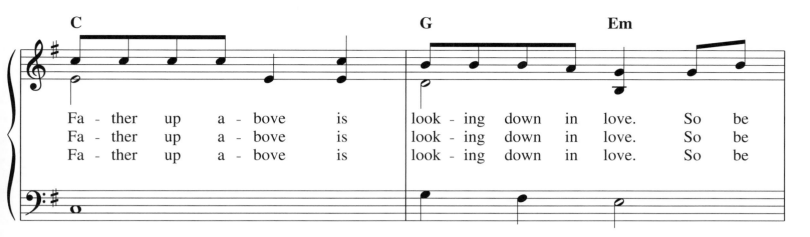

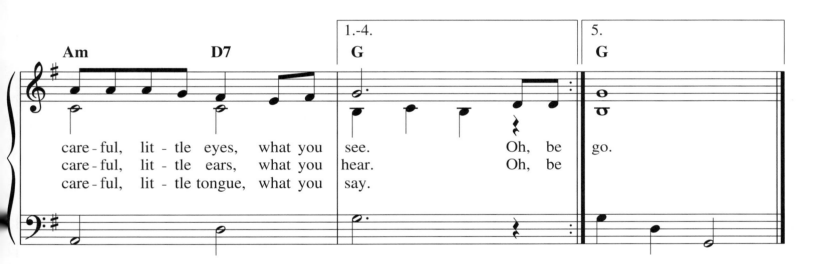

Additional Verses

4. Oh, be careful, little hands, what you do.
   Oh, be careful, little hands, what you do.
   For the Father up above is looking down in love.
   So be careful, little hands, what you do.

5. Oh, be careful, little feet, where you go.
   Oh, be careful, little feet, where you go.
   For the Father up above is looking down in love.
   So be careful, little feet, where you go.

PASS IT ON

Words and Music by
KURT KAISER

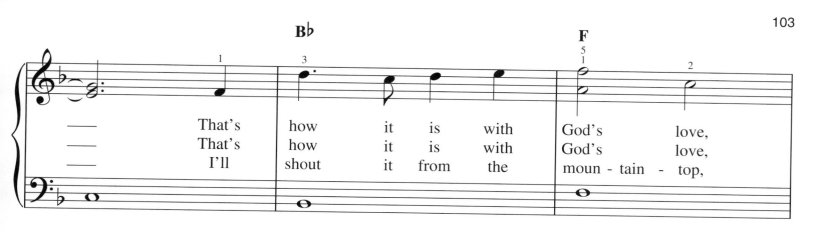

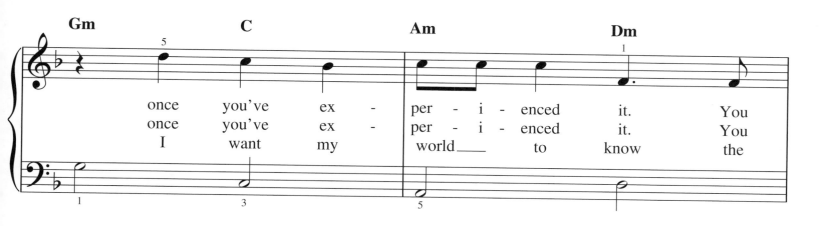

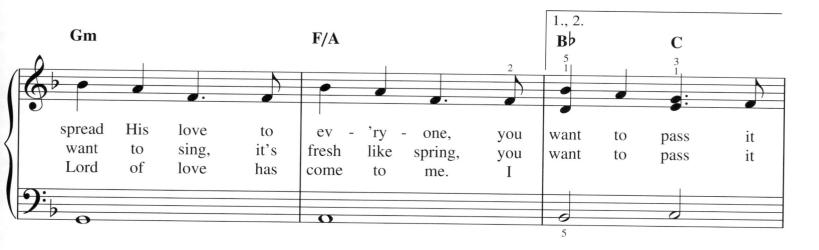

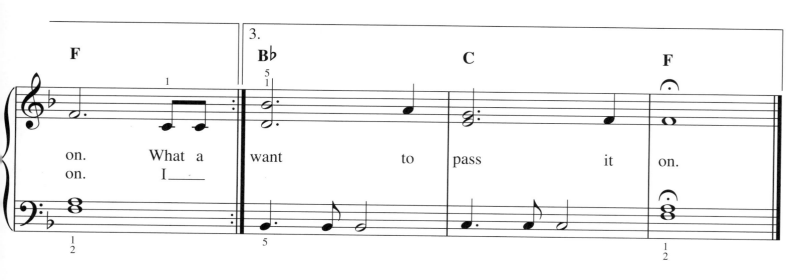

PRAISE HIM,
ALL YE LITTLE CHILDREN

Traditional Words
Music by CAREY BONNER

PRAISE THE NAME OF JESUS

Words and Music by
ROY HICKS, JR.

SEEK YE FIRST

Words and Music by
KAREN LAFFERTY

Gently, in 2

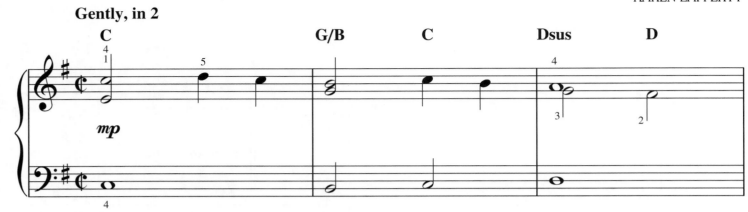

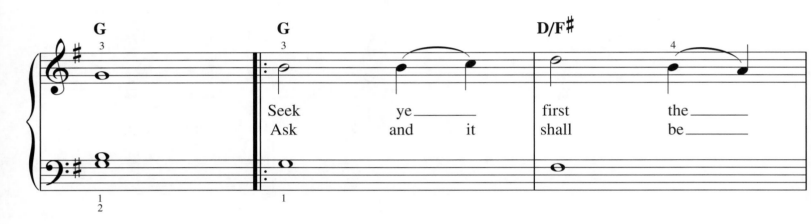

Seek ye_____ first the_____
Ask and it shall be_____

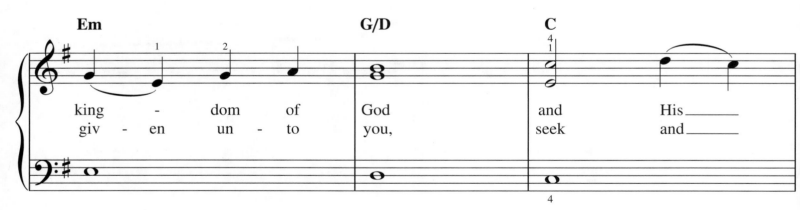

king - dom of God and His_____
giv - en un - to you, seek and_____

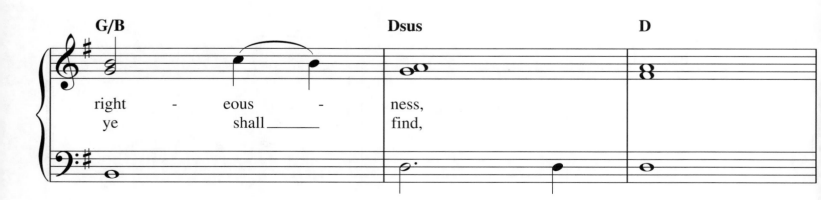

right - eous - ness,
ye shall_____ find,

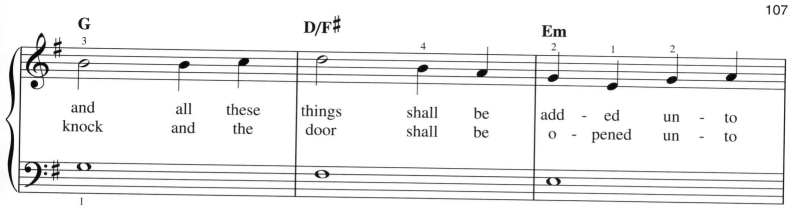

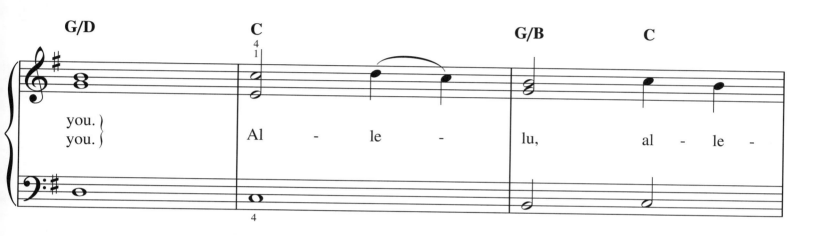

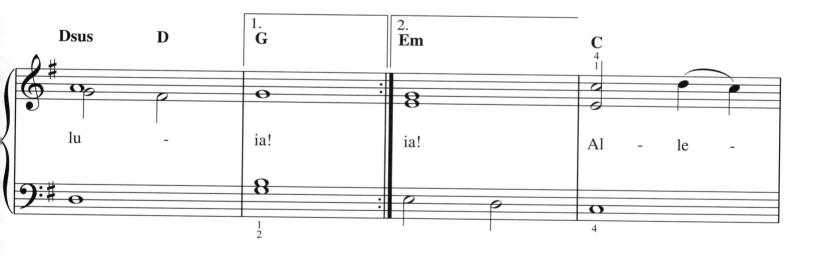

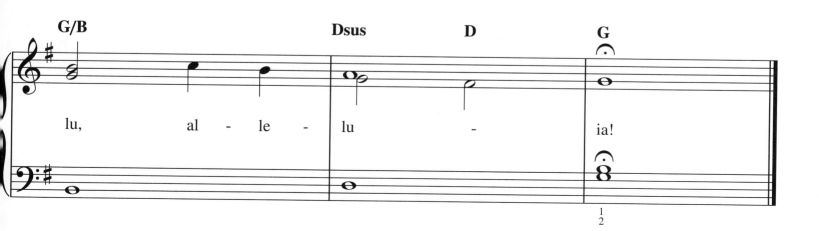

SING TO THE KING

Words and Music by
BILLY JAMES FOOTE

Moderately fast

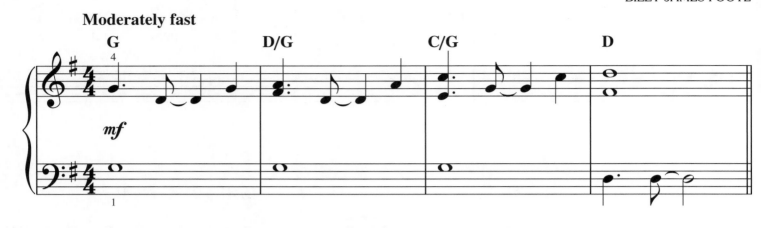

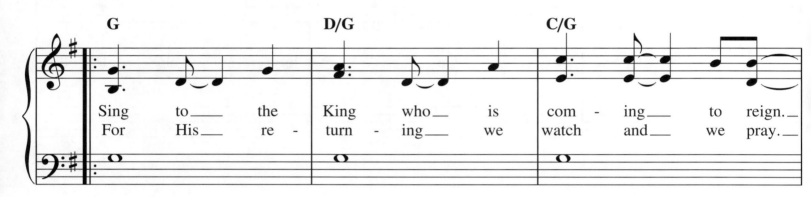

Sing to___ the King who___ is com - ing___ to reign.
For His___ re - turn - ing___ we watch and___ we pray.

Glo - ry___ to Je - sus,___ the
We will___ be read - y___ the

Lamb that___ was slain.
dawn of___ that day.

Life and___ sal -
We'll join___ in

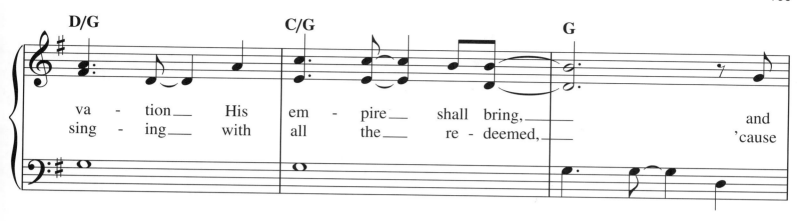
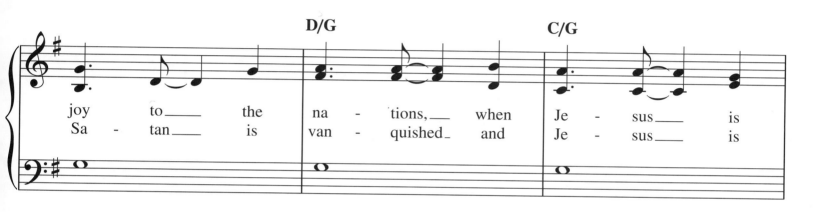

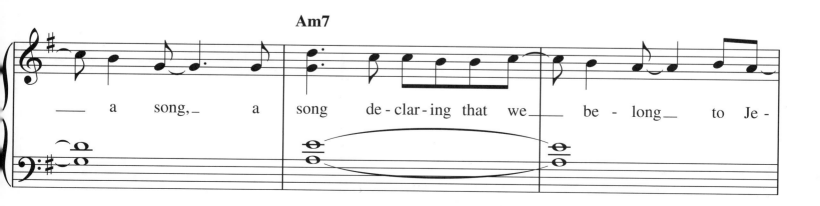

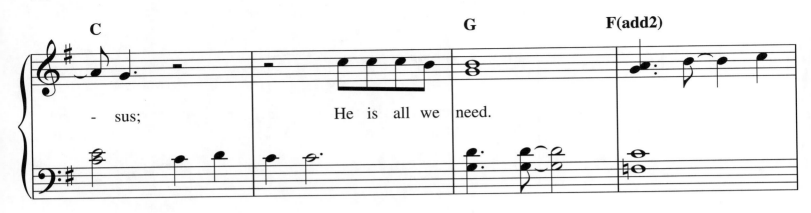

C **G** **F(add2)**

- sus; He is all we need.

G **Am7**

Lift up a heart of praise, sing now with voic-

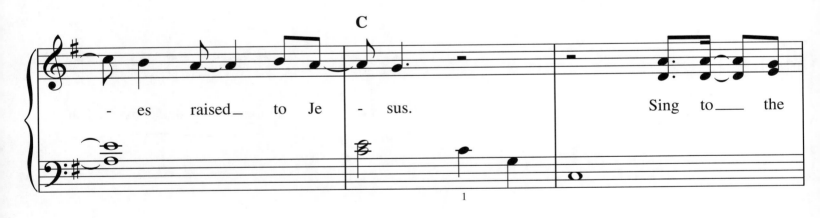

C

- es raised to Je - sus. Sing to the

G **1.** **D** **2.** **D** **G**

King.

STEP BY STEP

Words and Music by
DAVID STRASSER "BEAKER"

Moderately fast

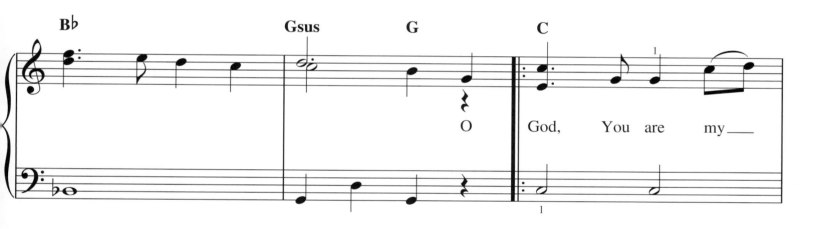

O God, You are my___

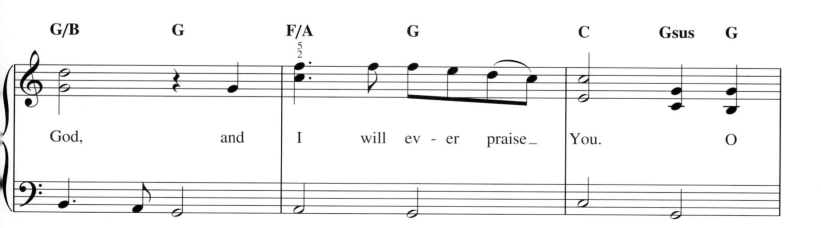

God,   and   I   will ev - er   praise_ You.   O

God, You are my___ God, and I will ev - er praise___

You. I will seek You in the morn-ing, and I will

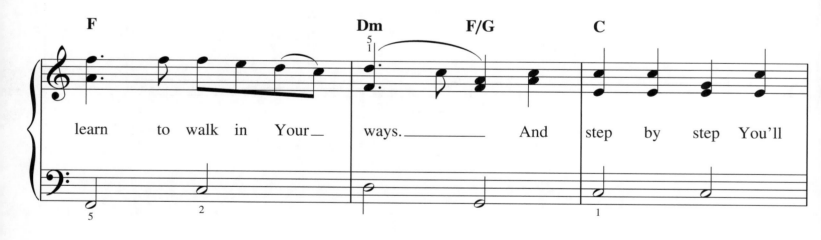

learn to walk in Your__ ways._____ And step by step You'll

lead me, and I will fol - low You all of my___

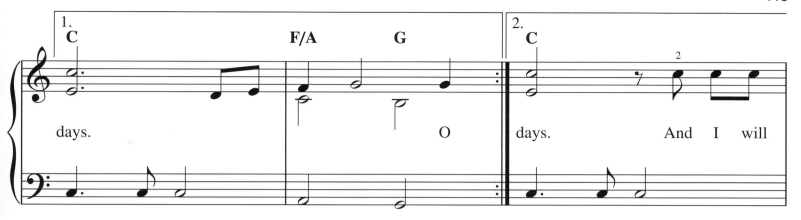

days.　　　　　　　O　days.　　And I will

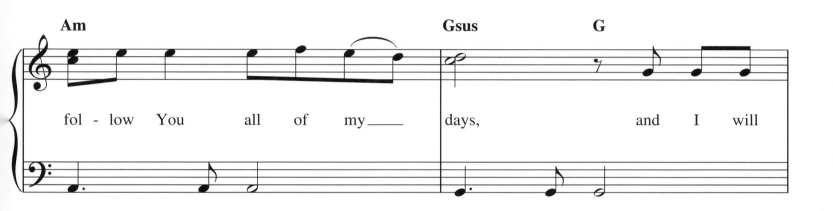

fol - low You　all　of　my___ days,　　and I will

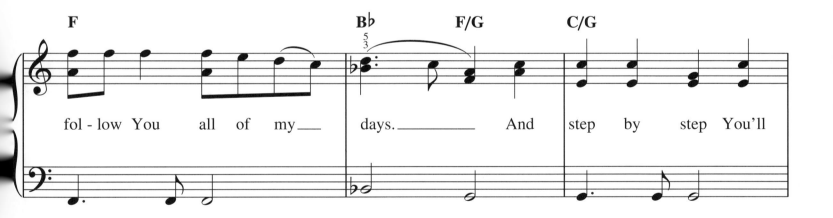

fol - low You　all　of　my___ days._____　And step by step You'll

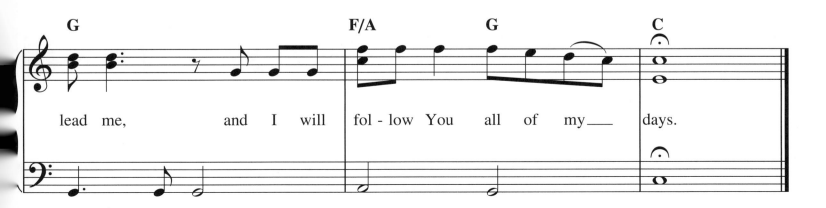

lead me,　　and I will　fol - low You　all　of　my___ days.

THANK YOU, LORD

Words and Music by PAUL BALOCHE
and DON MOEN

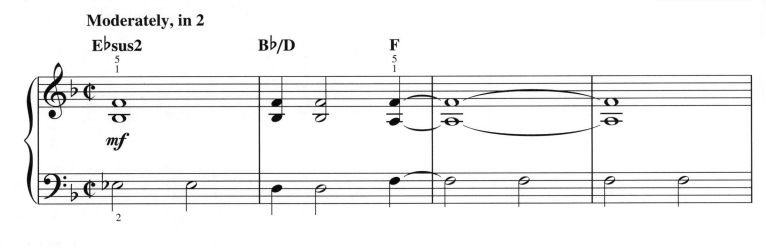

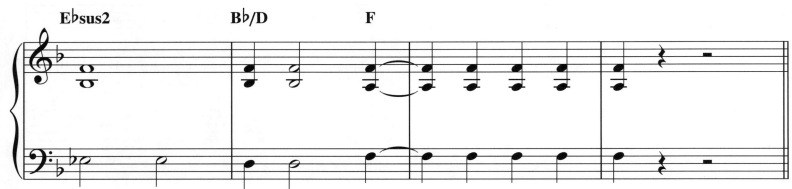

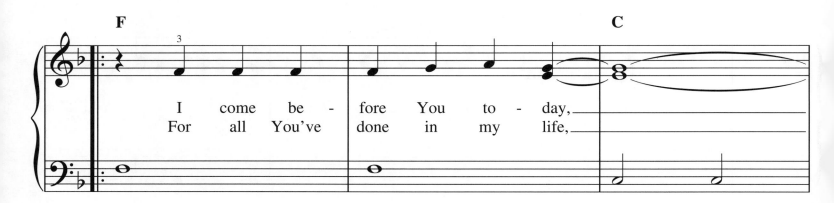

I come be - fore You to - day,
For all You've done in my day life,

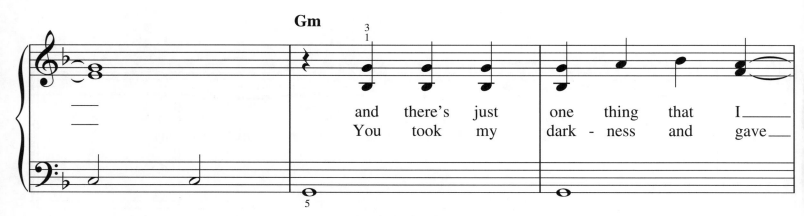

and there's just one thing that I
You took my dark - ness and gave

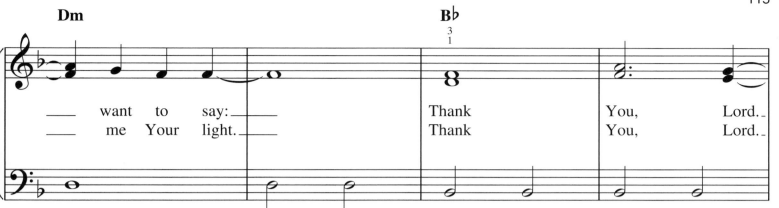

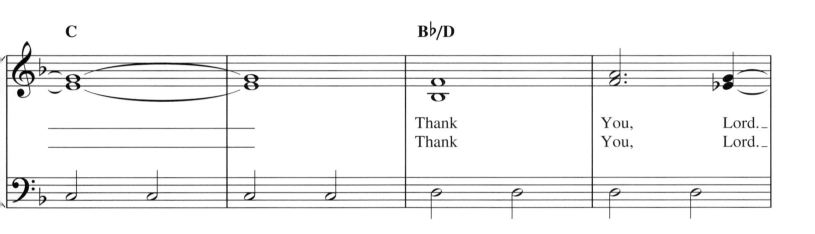

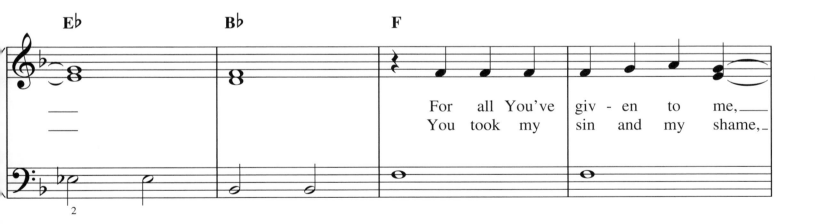

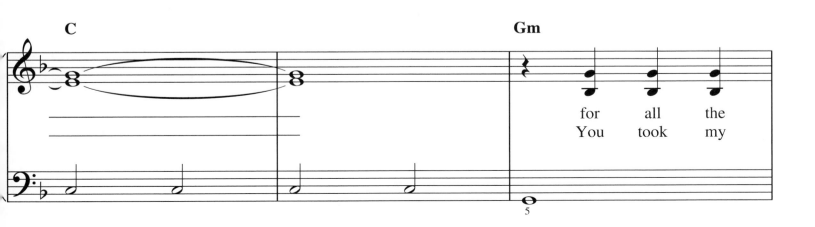

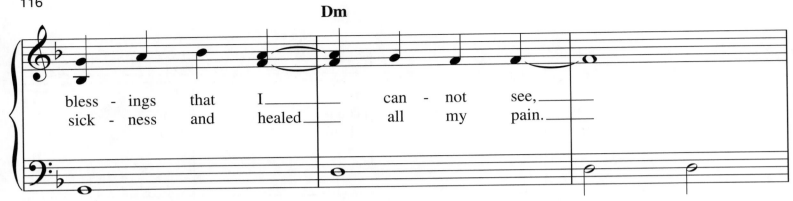

bless - ings that I ____ can - not see,____
sick - ness and healed ____ all my pain.____

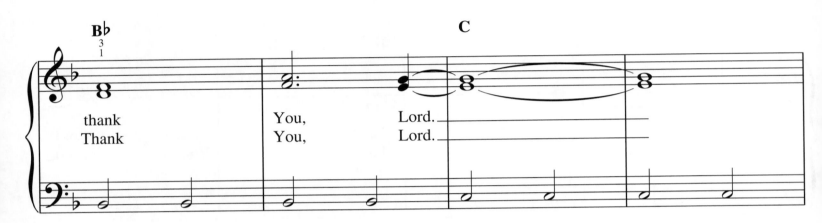

thank You, Lord.____
Thank You, Lord.____

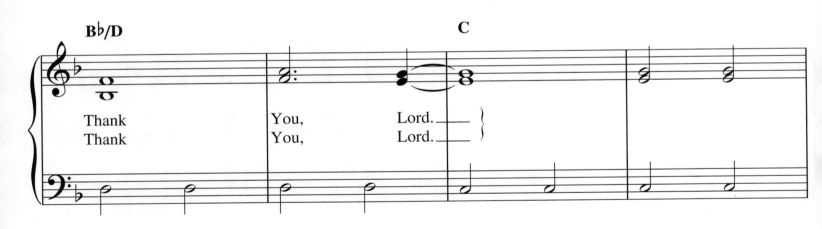

Thank You, Lord.____
Thank You, Lord.____

With a grate - ful heart, with a song of

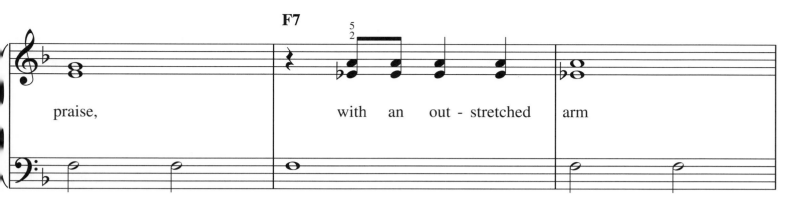

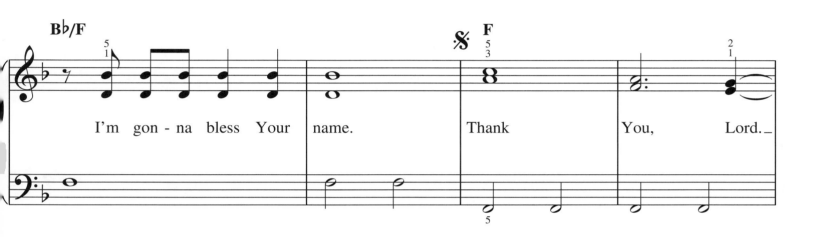

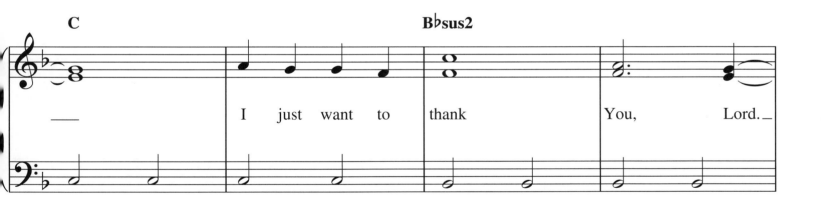

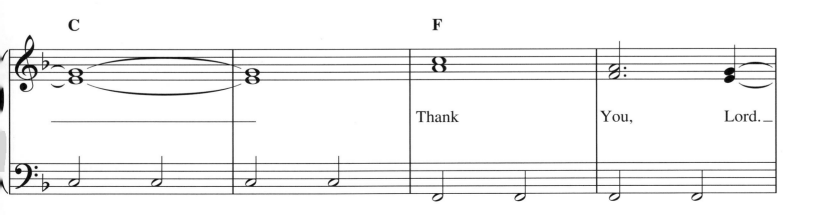

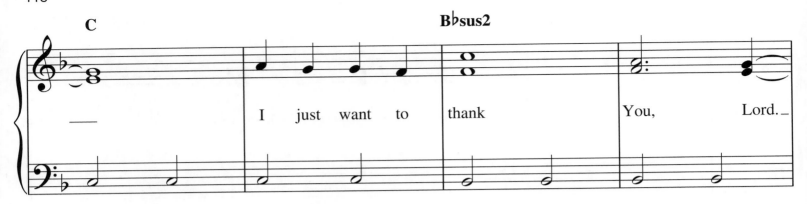

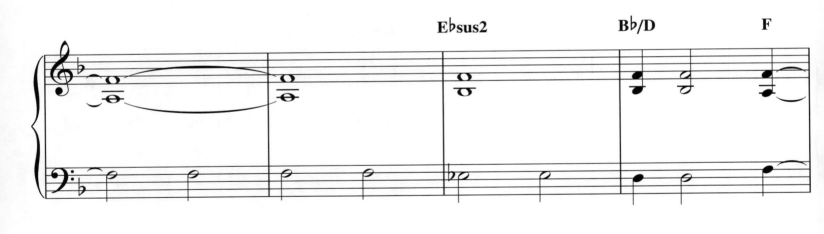

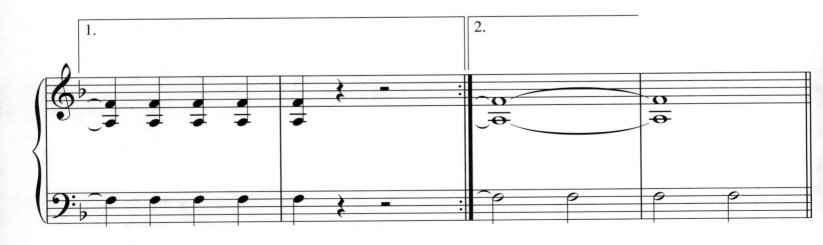

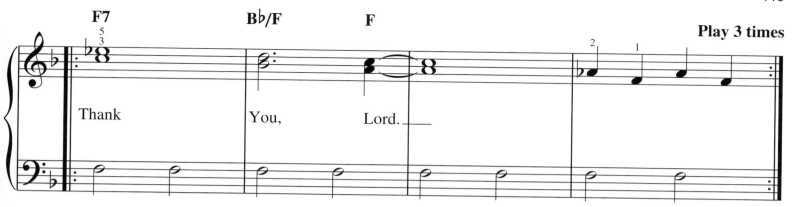

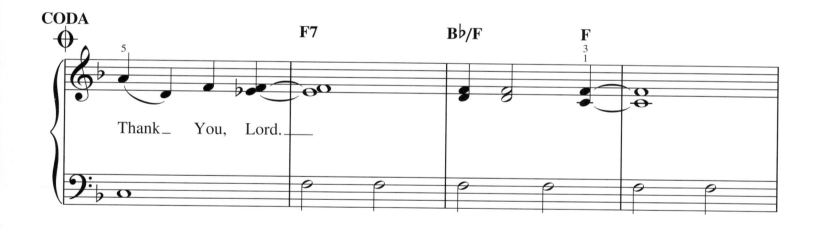

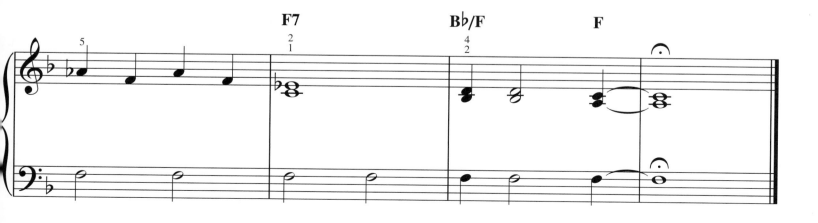

THERE IS A REDEEMER

Words and Music by
MELODY GREEN

Fa - ther, for giv - ing us Your Son,＿＿＿ and

To Coda ⊕

D.S. al Coda
(take 2nd ending)

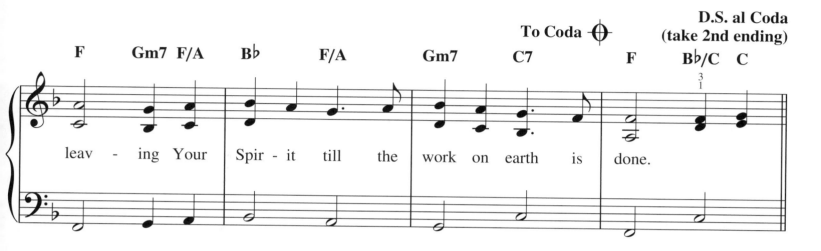

leav - ing Your Spir - it till the work on earth is done.

CODA

done. And leav - ing Your Spir - it till the

work＿ on＿ earth＿ is done.

THIS IS THE DAY

Words and Music by
LES GARRETT

THIS LITTLE LIGHT OF MINE

African-American Spiritual

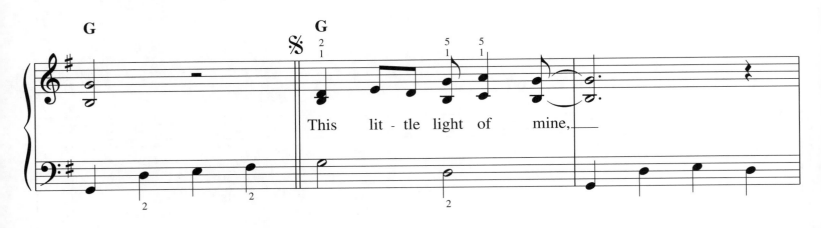

This lit - tle light of mine,

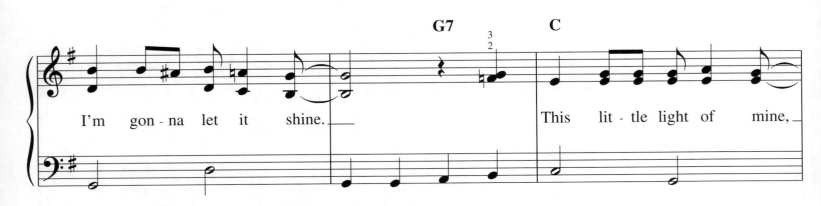

I'm gon - na let it shine.   This lit - tle light of mine,

I'm gon - na let it shine.

This lit - tle light of mine, I'm gon - na let it shine

ev - 'ry day, ev - 'ry day, ev - 'ry

day, ev - 'ry day gon - na let my lit - tle light

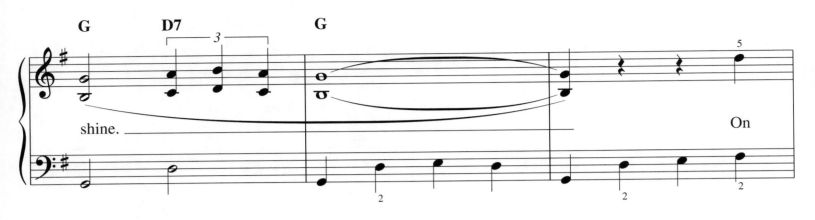

shine. _____ On

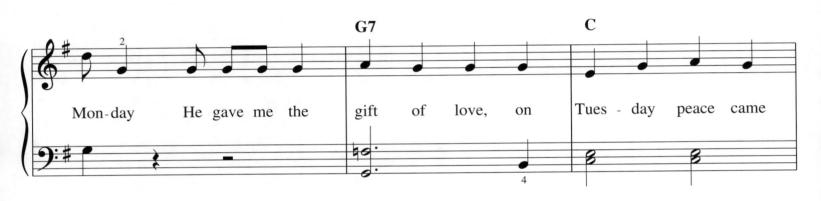

Mon-day He gave me the gift of love, on Tues - day peace came

from a - bove, on Wednes - day told me to have more faith, on

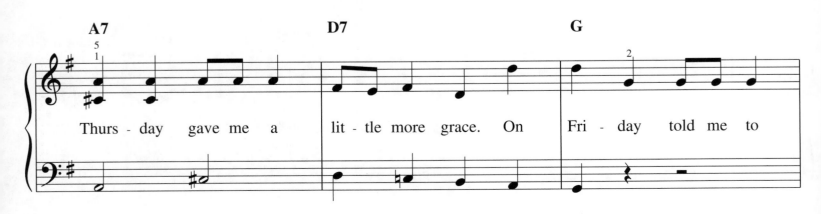

Thurs - day gave me a lit - tle more grace. On Fri - day told me to

127

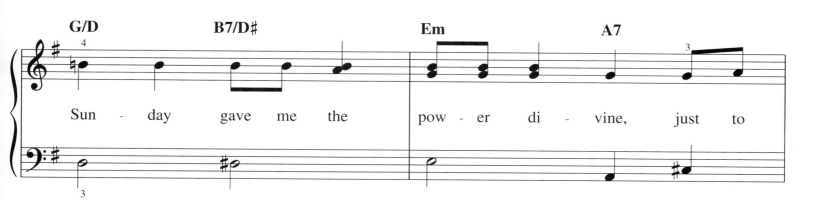

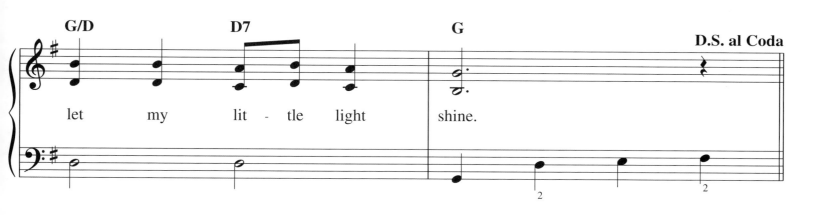

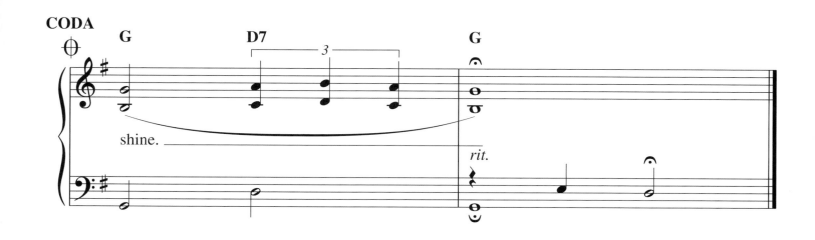

WHEN I AM AFRAID

Words and Music by
FRANK HERNANDEZ

Moderately slow

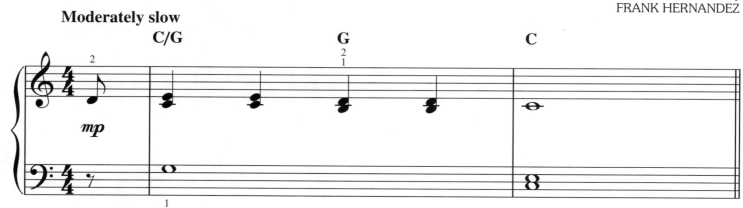

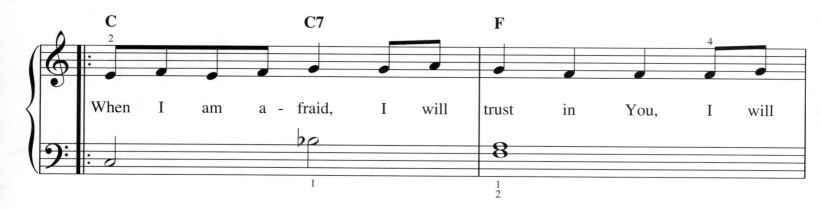

When I am a-fraid, I will trust in You, I will

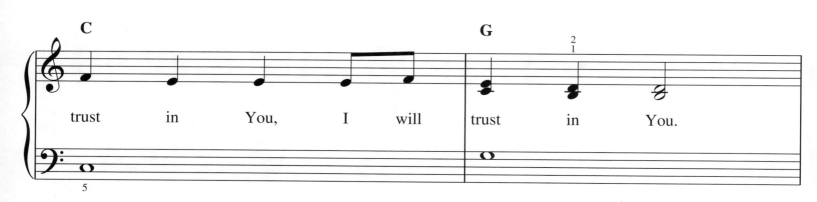

trust in You, I will trust in You.

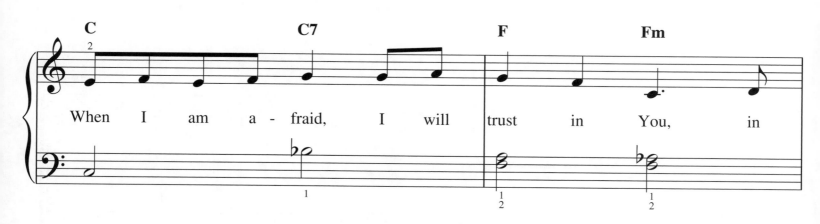

When I am a-fraid, I will trust in You, in

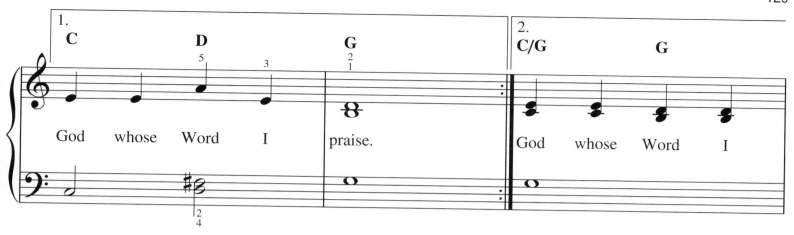

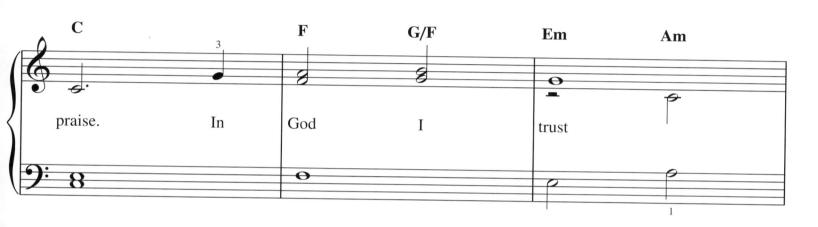

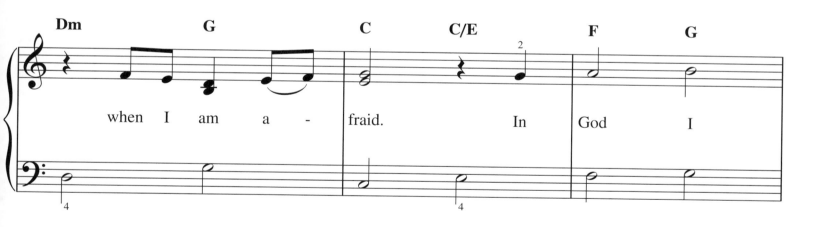

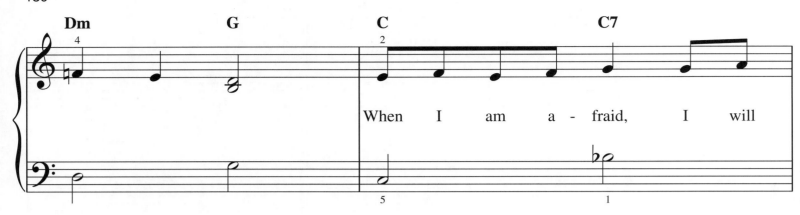

When I am a - fraid, I will

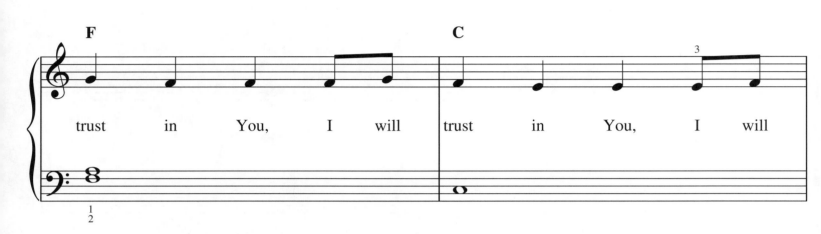

trust in You, I will trust in You, I will

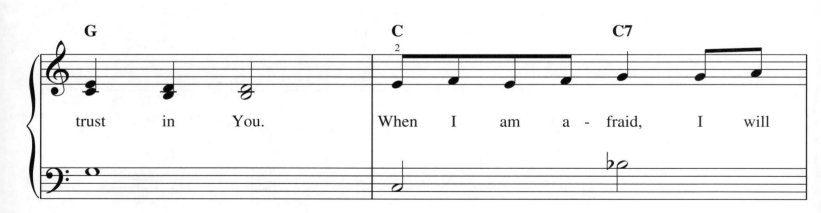

trust in You. When I am a - fraid, I will

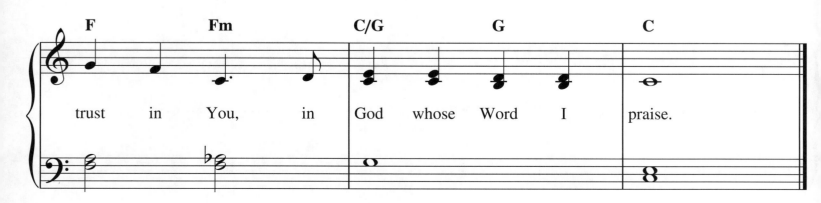

trust in You, in God whose Word I praise.

THE WISE MAN AND THE FOOLISH MAN

Traditional

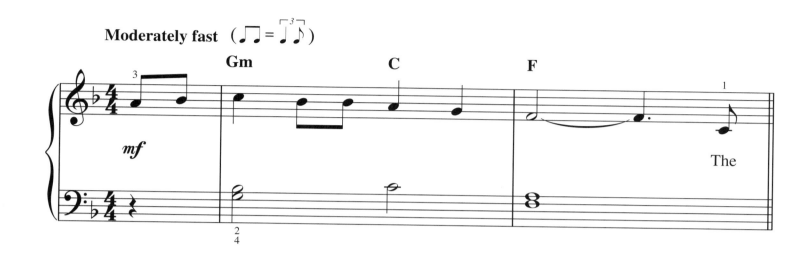

The

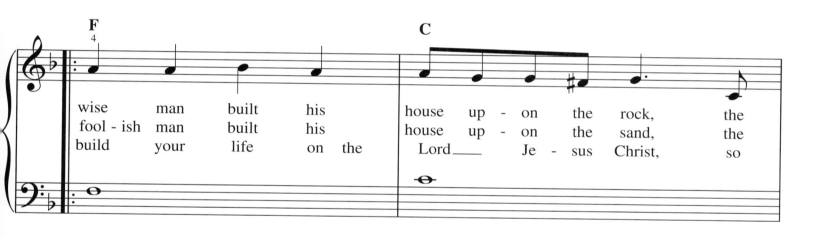

wise	man	built	his	house	up - on	the	rock,	the
fool - ish	man	built	his	house	up - on	the	sand,	the
build	your	life	on	the	Lord___	Je -	sus Christ,	so

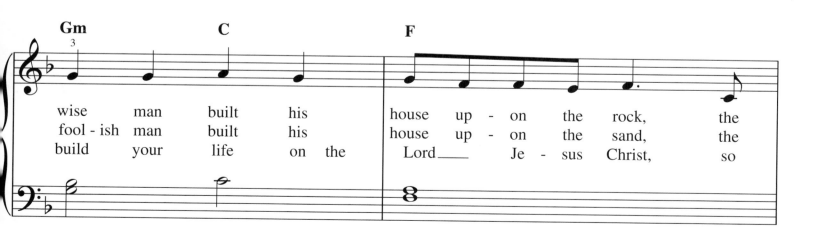

wise	man	built	his	house	up - on	the	rock,	the
fool - ish	man	built	his	house	up - on	the	sand,	the
build	your	life	on	the	Lord___	Je -	sus Christ,	so

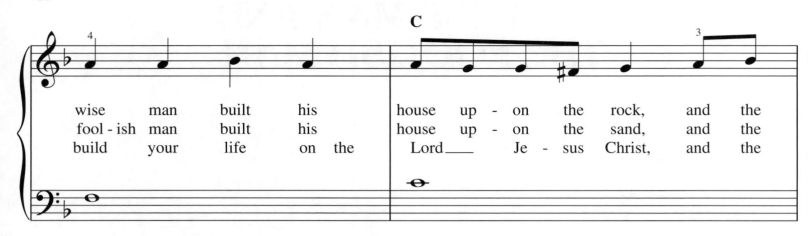

wise   man   built   his   house up - on   the   rock,   and   the
fool - ish man   built   his   house up - on   the   sand,   and   the
build   your   life   on the   Lord____   Je - sus Christ, and   the

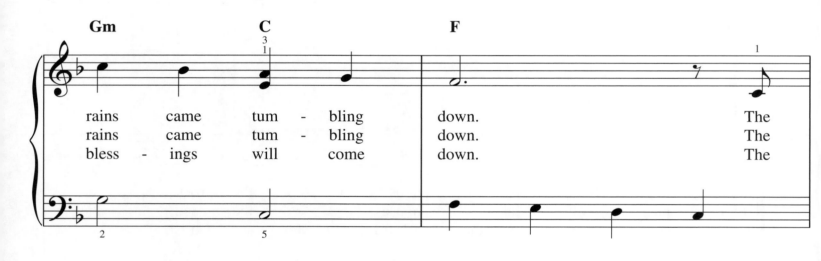

rains   came   tum - bling   down.   The
rains   came   tum - bling   down.   The
bless - ings will   come   down.   The

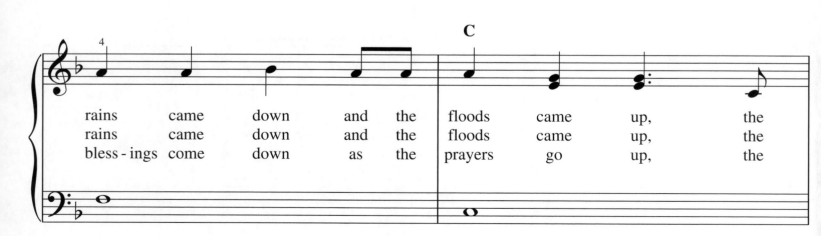

rains   came   down   and   the   floods came   up,   the
rains   came   down   and   the   floods came   up,   the
bless - ings come down   as   the   prayers go   up,   the

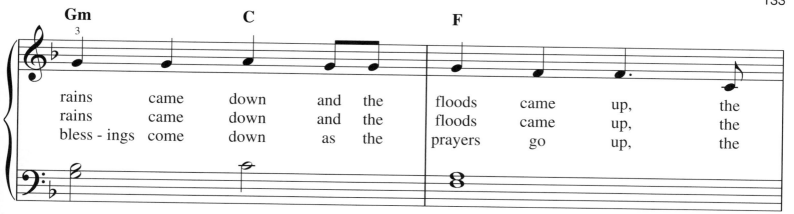

Gm   C   F

rains   came   down   and   the   floods   came   up,   the
rains   came   down   and   the   floods   came   up,   the
bless-ings come   down   as   the   prayers   go   up,   the

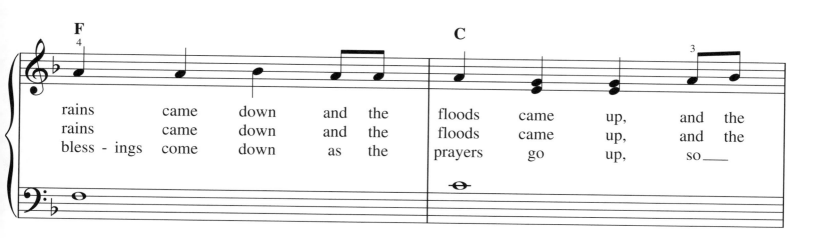

F   C

rains   came   down   and   the   floods   came   up,   and   the
rains   came   down   and   the   floods   came   up,   and   the
bless-ings come   down   as   the   prayers   go   up,   so___

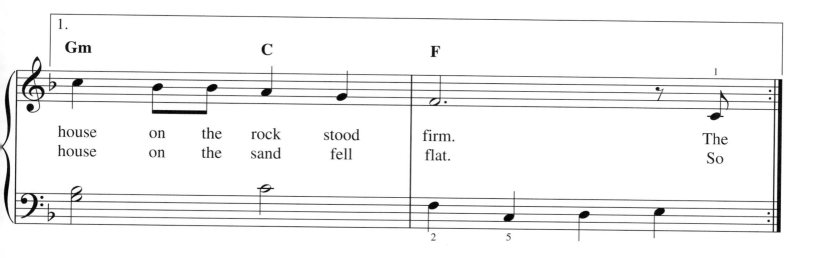

1.
Gm   C   F

house   on   the   rock   stood   firm.   The
house   on   the   sand   fell   flat.   So

3.
Gm   C   F

build   your   life   on   the   Lord.

ZACCHAEUS

Traditional

Zac - chae - us was a
chae - us knew that

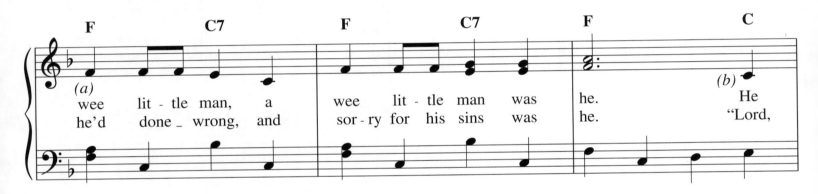

(a)
wee lit - tle man, a wee lit - tle man was he. (b) He
he'd done _ wrong, and sor - ry for his sins was he. "Lord,

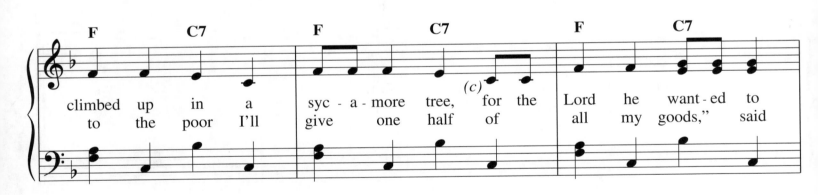

climbed up in a syc - a - more tree, (c) for the Lord he want - ed to
to the poor I'll give one half of all my goods," said

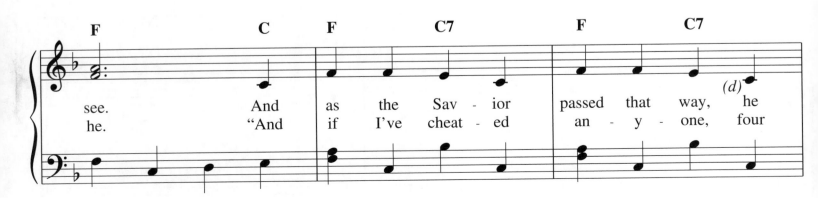

see. And as the Sav - ior passed that way, he (d)
he. "And if I've cheat - ed an - y - one, four

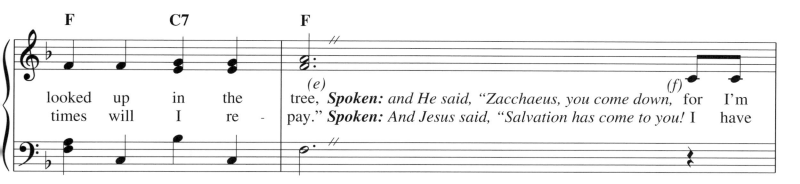

looked   up   in   the   tree, **Spoken:** *and He said, "Zacchaeus, you come down,* for I'm
times   will   I   re -   pay." **Spoken:** *And Jesus said, "Salvation has come to you! I* have

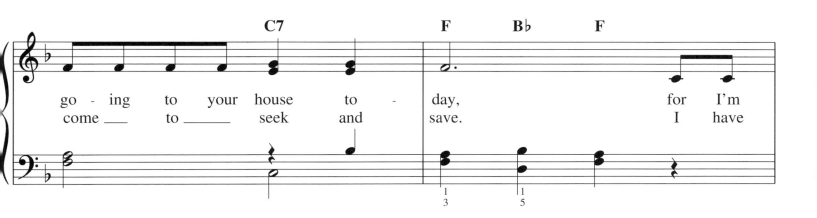

go - ing   to   your   house   to - day,   for   I'm
come ___ to ___ seek   and   save.   I   have

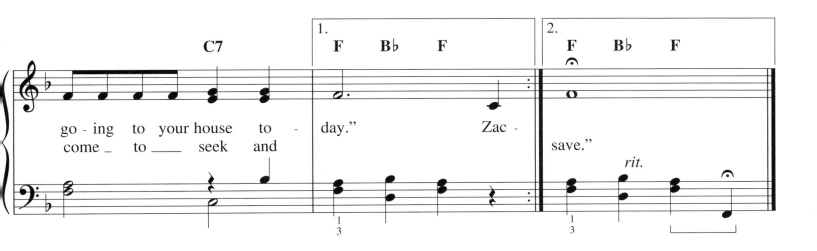

go - ing   to your house   to - day."   Zac -
come _ to ___ seek   and   save."

Motions for Verse 1:

(a) *Hands in front, right palm raised above left palm.*
(b) *Alternate hands in climbing motion.*
(c) *Shade eyes with right hand and look down.*
(d) *Shade eyes with right hand and look up.*
(e) *Speak these words while looking up and beckoning with hand.*
(f) *Clap hands on beats 1 and 3 until end of Verse 1.*

The Best Praise & Worship
Songbooks for Piano

Above All
THE PHILLIP KEVEREN SERIES

15 beautiful praise song piano solo arrangements, perfect for home or congregational use. Includes: Agnus Dei • Ancient of Days • Breathe • Draw Me Close • I Stand in Awe • I Want to Know You • More Love, More Power • Step by Step • We Fall Down • more.

00311024 Piano Solo...............................$11.95

The Best of Worship Together®

15 super-popular worship songs: Forever • He Reigns • Here I Am to Worship • Let Everything That Has Breath • and more.

00306635 P/V/G.....................................$14.95
00311143 Easy Piano $9.95

The Best Praise & Worship Songs Ever

80 all-time favorites: Breathe • Days of Elijah • Here I Am to Worship • I Could Sing of Your Love Forever • Open the Eyes of My Heart • Shout to the Lord • We Bow Down • dozens more.

00311057 P/V/G.....................................$19.95

The Best Praise & Worship Songs Ever – Easy Piano

Over 70 of the best P&W songs today, including: Awesome God • Blessed Be Your Name • Days of Elijah • Here I Am to Worship • Open the Eyes of My Heart • Shout to the Lord • We Fall Down • and more.

00311312 Easy Piano $19.95

Here I Am to Worship

30 top songs from such CCM stars as Rebecca St. James, Matt Redman, and others. Includes: Be Glorified • Enough • It Is You • Let My Words Be Few • Majesty • We Fall Down • You Alone • more.

00313270 P/V/G.....................................$14.95

Here I Am to Worship – For Kids

This great songbook lets the kids join in on 20 of the best modern worship songs, including: God of Wonders • He Is Exalted • The Heart of Worship • Song of Love • Wonderful Maker • and more.

00316098 Easy Piano $14.95

I Could Sing of Your Love Forever
THE PHILLIP KEVEREN SERIES

15 worship songs arranged for solo piano: Holy Ground • I Could Sing of Your Love Forever • I Love You Lord • In This Very Room • My Utmost for His Highest • The Potter's Hand • The Power of Your Love • Shout to the North • more.

00310905 Piano Solo...............................$12.95

Modern Worship
THE CHRISTIAN MUSICIAN SERIES

35 favorites of contemporary congregations, including: All Things Are Possible • Ancient of Days • The Heart of Worship • Holiness • I Could Sing of Your Love Forever • I Will Exalt Your Name • It Is You • We Fall Down • You Are My King (Amazing Love) • and more.

00310957 P/V/G.....................................$14.95

Shout to the Lord!
THE PHILLIP KEVEREN SERIES

Moving arrangements of 14 praise song favorites, including: As the Deer • Great Is the Lord • More Precious than Silver • Oh Lord, You're Beautiful • Shine, Jesus, Shine • Shout to the Lord • Thy Word • and more.

00310699 Piano Solo...............................$12.95

Timeless Praise
THE PHILLIP KEVEREN SERIES

20 songs of worship arranged for easy piano by Phillip Keveren: El Shaddai • Give Thanks • How Beautiful • How Majestic Is Your Name • Oh Lord, You're Beautiful • People Need the Lord • Seek Ye First • There Is a Redeemer • Thy Word • and more.

00310712 Easy Piano $12.95

Worship Together® Favorites

All Over the World • Cry Out to Jesus • Empty Me • Everlasting God • Forever • Happy Day • Holy Is the Lord • How Deep the Father's Love for Us • How Great Is Our God • Indescribable • Join the Song • Ready for You • Wholly Yours • Yes You Have • You Never Let Go.

00313360 P/V/G.....................................$16.95

Worship Together® Favorites for Kids

Enough • Everlasting God • Forever • From the Inside Out • Holy Is the Lord • How Great Is Our God • Made to Worship • Mountain of God • Wholly Yours • The Wonderful Cross • Yes You Have • You Never Let Go.

00316109 Easy Piano $12.95

Worship Together® Platinum

22 of the best contemporary praise & worship songs: Be Glorified • Better Is One Day • Draw Me Close • Every Move I Make • Here I Am to Worship • I Could Sing of Your Love Forever • O Praise Him (All This for a King) • and more.

00306721 P/V/G.....................................$16.95

Worship – The Ultimate Collection

Matching folio with 24 top worship favorites, including: God of Wonders • He Reigns • Hungry (Falling on My Knees) • Lord, Reign in Me • Open the Eyes of My Heart • Yesterday, Today and Forever • and more.

00313337 P/V/G.....................................$17.95

FOR MORE INFORMATION, SEE YOUR LOCAL MUSIC DEALER,
OR WRITE TO:

HAL•LEONARD®
CORPORATION
7777 W. BLUEMOUND RD. P.O. BOX 13819 MILWAUKEE, WI 53213

For complete song lists and to view our entire catalog of titles, please visit www.halleonard.com

Prices, contents, and availability subject to change without notice.